The Secret World of
SHLOMO FINE

K.M.R. Smythe

The Secret World of
SHLOMO FINE

ISBN 978-0-7974-9135-9
EAN 9780797491359
Copyright © K.M.R. Smythe

AmaguguPublishers

Published in 2018
Published by Amagugu Publishers
Typeset & designed by Kudzai Chikomo

The moral right of the author has been asserted.

This is primarily a book of memory and memory has its own story to tell. It reflects the author's experience of a particular time and place in the past; some names and characteristics have been changed, some events have been compressed and some dialogue has been recreated. The author has sought and been given permission to include the memories of others in this work.

Distributed by African Books Collective

www.amagugupublishers.com

For my children with love

In memory of my mother and my father

Dedicated to Ntete, Marupa, Mapicke and Gonrogh

With loving gratitude to Lea

Special thanks to Pathisa and Fikile Nyathi

If you hide painful stories, they become more painful.
Sathnam Sanghera

Events do not follow a script. This is being human.
Naoki Higashida – A young man's voice from the silence of autism

Prologue

"How's Champie?" My father's sunburnt face greeted me from his place at the head of the table. "Fine," I replied as I pulled my chair closer in. My bare feet tingled. I'd sprinted across the hot sand on the driveway. The black granolith steps into the house had soaked up the midday sun and fried the soles of my feet. "Ja, good old Champ hey," my father said as he shook out his serviette. I'd heard the bell for Sunday lunch while I sat high up in my favourite tree near the tennis court. I suddenly felt light-headed from coming in out of the raging heat. Hunger welled up inside me and saliva flooded my mouth.

Martha, wearing her starched Sunday whites, wheeled the trolley into the dining room. The incessant singing of cicadas outside the window filled the stillness. All eyes scanned the dishes arranged on the top and the bottom of the trolley. With gloved hands, Martha lifted up the roasted chicken on its silver salver and put it in front of my mother. While my mother carved, Martha pushed the trolley round the table, stopping to spoon steaming vegetables onto our plates. John was reminded by my mother that one wing bone was for me. Martha placed the plate of sliced chicken onto the trolley and went around to each of us once more. I signalled vigorously to her not to spoil my crisply roasted potatoes and the pile of fried bread and onion stuffing that my mother had taught her to make, by dousing them with gravy. She dutifully watered the chicken slices on my plate with enough brown sauce to make them all but disappear. This was followed by a sizeable dollop of bread sauce that wallowed in the gravy like a milky island.

My father's voice droned on about people I didn't know or care about. My mother made interested noises as I picked my way through my food. After a second helping of potatoes, I fiddled with my fork and pushed coagulated bread sauce around with my knife, peas and carrots stealthily hidden underneath its rubbery mass.

John's hand creeping under the table caught my eye. I swatted at him as he fed bits of chicken to the bulldog that rested its doleful head on his lap. John told me to stop being a spoil sport and I said he better watch out after lunch if he didn't stop being such a pest. "For heaven's sakes, can't you just be happy for one minute and finish what you're eating Caitriona!" my mother snapped. Monique flicked me with her serviette and I got hold of it and flicked her back. Monique wrestled her serviette back from my grasp with a grunt. The cicadas' ringing made the hollow impasse between us sting with contempt. My mother glared at me.

"You'll miss me when I'm gone!" I muttered, thinking about the forthcoming tennis tournament in Salisbury. My mother made a humphing noise as she reached over for the silver bell.

Martha came and took our plates away. John drummed his fingers on the table while Martha wheeled in the apple pie. Monique said she was on a diet. My father said "Looks like old Martha here is the one who needs to be on a diet I reckon" and he gave one of his snorty laughs. My mother gave him a dark look and whispered "Norman!" Monique stuffed her starched serviette into its silver ring with 'MF' engraved on it in swirly letters. She sat back in her chair to examine her pointed red finger nails. I gazed with envy at the dress ring on her middle finger, its pom-pom of lime green and hot pink sequins fizzing with a feminine charm that I yearned to be mine too. I vowed to myself that it was time to quit biting my nails. I looked at the ragged and bloodied ends of my fingers and knew that this wasn't going to happen any time soon.

My mother said she'd asked Shareen to stop calling me 'Caitie'. She said she and my father had specifically chosen names for us that couldn't be shortened or messed about with. My father clearly seemed to have forgotten about not messing with anyone's names. He called Martha a 'bladdy clueless kaffir' when she spilled the custard on the tablecloth.

PART ONE

We remember what we want to forget and we forget what we want to
remember.
Cormac McCarthy

We can look away from a face, but we cannot escape the sound of an
emotion. We teach our children to inhibit the unpleasant sounds
associated with some emotions, especially the terrible cries of
despair and agony.
Paul Ekman

(top to bottom, left to right) Mary holding John, John and myself with Margaret
and Tiger the bulldog,
Anderson standing outside the little house, my mother with John and myself (the
women's ward is visible behind the hedge), me wearing a white party dress, me
cuddling a hug-a-bug,
my mother with John on the lower lawn at the superintendent's house,
me sitting next to the fish pond with an inmate in the background,
Hardy the bulldog standing on the top lawn in front of the veranda.

1

On 2nd December 1952 my parents, Lesley aged five and Monique aged three, climbed on board the Edinburgh Castle at Southampton and sailed to Africa. When the ship docked in Cape Town, my parents were met by Richard Boschoff from the World Health Organisation who gave my father further information about his new post. They then travelled by train to Bulawayo in Southern Rhodesia for my father, Dr. Norman Fine, to take up his position at Ingutsheni Mental Hospital. Norman started working there on 3rd January 1953.

I was born on the 12th of July 1955. My mother said it took ages for me to arrive and that when I finally did, I was very red in the face. My father came to see me at the Mater Dei Hospital soon after I was born. My mother said he took one look at me and exclaimed "Ah 'sweet Cait' – let's call her Cait!" My mother wrote:

> *"Lesley and Monique were interested in you – Monique used to push your pram around – she dressed up like a nun, with her skipping rope around her waist! But on the whole they didn't do much with you as a tiny baby – they were both at school (full time) and had afternoon activities, etc., etc. so you were very much my baby. They were not at all jealous of you – having their own interests and friends. Monique was six and Lesley seven when you were born. They thought you were cute and they enjoyed the breastfeeding – if you cried for any reason, they were sure you were hungry! Gave me instructions to 'give her a nibble!' Norman did not participate in any toilet training, but he worried and was upset by your determination to live on rice krispies for ever, and insisted that you ate other things – he fed you in spite of your resistance. We had disagreements over this, because I never had any difficulties with Lesley or Monique..."*

In 1956 we moved from Matsheumhlope to live in a bungalow in the grounds of Ingutsheni. Our new home was diagonally over the road from the female ward, and around the corner from the administration block where my father had his office. My mother was pregnant when we moved and my brother John was born in 1957.

I could hear the inmates through the hibiscus hedge that separated our house from the wards. Sometimes John and I would creep into the hedge and sit inside it, trying to see who was screaming. We could see an exercise yard surrounded by iron bars that were made in the shape of long legged birds like flamingos. It seemed as if the birds were responsible for the racket behind them. Occasionally we caught sight of a bedraggled grey head or a pair of feet shuffling along in fluffy slippers. Other times a person would hang onto the bars and make such horrible noises that we ran off to hide inside the house. They made screeches like the grey lowrie birds whose harsh voices called *'gwaa gwaa'* - 'go away, go away' or like the black crows that squawked at each other from the top of the rubber hedge and dive bombed my father's white Mini when he drove around the corner to his office.

By all accounts I was not an easy child. My family remember me as having a short fuse. Lesley remembers how John and I got on her nerves by screaming at each other when she was trying to concentrate on her homework. My mother inscribed The Complete Works of Shakespeare with a quote from The Taming of the Shrew – *"To Cait of Cait Hall, super dainty Cait"* - when she gave it to me for my twenty fifth birthday, so I guess my temper made a lasting impression on her too. Lesley said I was a pest, always fighting with John and arguing with Monique, until I was given a hiding or sent to my room. Meal times were very dull. My parents shared gossip about their medical friends and my father talked endlessly about psychiatric conditions as though the world revolved around him and his encyclopaedic knowledge. Occasionally, when my mother gave one or other of our servants a day off, she would cook us a roast with all the trimmings. At the end of the meal, my father would throw his serviette onto the table next to his empty plate and say "That was excellent Elsa. Did Anderson cook it?" My mother would click her tongue and look annoyed.

My mother Elspeth seldom swore and hardly ever shouted. She had shown great promise as a ballerina in her teens. She combined her elegant dress sense with shoes and a handbag that matched her chosen colour scheme. She was never without a petticoat and a pearl necklace to complete her outfit. She would gracefully do the splits when asked to do so, even though her joints made clicking and cracking noises as she lowered herself to the floor. She used to remind me that she won the hurdles at her sports days when she was my age. She said that if she'd been a boy she'd have got a scholarship to attend a grammar school. My mother was clearly bright enough to have gone to university but this was not so readily encouraged in 1934 when she was eighteen.

My father bore a vague resemblance to the actor David Niven in the earliest photographs I have of him. I've only got three photos of him before he became my father. One is an official portrait of him wearing his Medical Officer's uniform during the war, and I've studied his twinkling gaze and his little moustache a million times at least. He kept his hands neatly manicured and his grey hair bryl-creamed into place. His speech was sprinkled with Afrikaans words like 'hekkies' for pimples and *'guti'* for the damp mist that sometimes clouded around trees on cold winter mornings. He liked to laugh at his own jokes, especially the names he came up with for people he disliked, or even people he liked; it was hard to tell because that's what he did most of the time. My father's favourite hobby was cleaning the nicotine out of his cigarette holder with a pipe cleaner. I always gave him pipe cleaners for his birthday because that's what my mother said he liked best. He breathed heavily as he concentrated on it, oblivious of the stench and the gunk he shunted into his silver ash tray. Besides his Old Spice Aftershave, that's the smell I associate most strongly with him.

***

My love affair with animals began when I was a very young child. There is a photograph of me and John sitting on the black granolith steps which led into the front garden. Next to us is our African nanny Margaret and she's holding a brindle bulldog against her lap. The dog is the one smiling at the camera.

I have scant memories of a Siamese cat named Sinbad. Some of my earliest photographs show him being petted by me and John on the front lawn. Besides his black and white markings I remember he had a pair of piercing blue eyes and a high pitched voice. I have stronger memories of a tabby cat that came to live in the back of the garage, in amongst some dusty old sacks. She was named Mother Pussy after she gave birth to a squirming litter of kittens. I remember my mother guiding my fingers across the expansive mound of Mother Pussy's stomach so that I could feel them moving underneath her skin. I can still see those delightful kittens with their newly opened blue eyes and their little pointy tails as they staggered and played around their dozing mother. I remember their ecstasy as they kneaded and purred and mewled over her, together with the sweet smell of milk and freshly licked fur as they lay together in the musty sunlight. My father took to calling me "Little Miss Pussy" after he noticed my joy at cradling the kittens in my arms and carting them about the garden. And so it was a total horror when I found all the kittens dead one day in the garage and Mother Pussy gone and lost to me forever. My mother said a wild dog had got into the garage. My father said that he had caught Mother Pussy eating her own dead kittens and so he had chased her away. I started to have nightmares of headless kittens trying to find me and keep me company. That was something that plagued me for quite a long time.

***

My birthday was in the middle of winter and it coincided with the circus coming to town. I remember the magical moment of going inside the big creamy canvas tent with its golden sawdust ring as if it was yesterday. The ring was warm and welcoming compared to the bone dry surroundings of the bush at Ingutsheni and the deadened grasses that grew alongside the roads that went into the city centre. Winter nights were ice cold and early morning frosts burned the grass, including our lawn, to a grey and lifeless carpet. I sat between my parents and watched the elephants chasing along, holding onto each other's tails with their trunks. It was a comical and harmless thing to see such huge animals being so obedient. I was captivated by the white circus horses, and I loved the way they bowed their heads and snorted as they cantered around the ring. At the crack of a whip, they jumped, or trotted or stood to attention with their front legs waving to me in the audience. They didn't miss a beat when girls in tutus jumped onto their backs and did acrobatic things. I remember how the sequins on their costumes sparkled, how the girls' bright faces beamed and how the horses seemed content to gallop gently around in circles. I held my breath as the acrobats swung upside down above us. To the roll of drums, they flew through the air and I sat mesmerised with a mixture of fear and delight as they saved each other from plummeting down to earth.

My mother took me and John to watch the show jumping and dressage at the Trade Fair in the Bulawayo Show Grounds. I sat on the edge of my seat and willed each rider over the jumps. I made jumps around the garden and John galloped along behind me. We strung pieces of string between garden chairs and made courses around the lawn. We jumped over everything – the stone walls along the flower beds, in and out of the concrete sandpit under the thatched shelter, through the water sprinkler, and up and down the corridors of the house. A terrible tragedy put paid to my show-jumping attendance when a honey-coloured horse tripped over a jump, broke its leg and had to be shot.

***

I started at Junior School in 1959 and my first teacher, Mrs Mackay, read us Robert Louis Stevenson's poetry. I dreamed of having a horse that I would name Counterpane, who would gallop me around the bush at Ingutsheni, all the way to school and back home again. When I was about seven, my mother took me to see Albert Lamorisse's film about a stallion called White Mane. I remember how the boy in the film befriended a wild horse and rode it into the waves away from a bunch of horrible men who had tried to catch it with ropes and break its spirit. I so wanted to be that boy on that stallion because the film ended with them going to live on an island where children and animals stayed friends forever.

It was around that time in my life that we got a black and white television. My father was forever fiddling with its aerial to stop the picture from turning into fuzzy lines. I longed to have a horse like the Lone Ranger's one called Silver that would come when I whistled and help me do good works with a Red Indian friend like Tonto.

***

I remember occasionally finding the desiccated remains of a guinea pig in the rubber hedge. I don't know what became of Sinbad the cat or all the budgies that used to chatter so insistently in the mornings. I used to laugh at a story my mother read me about a donkey who had a bad look in his eye. She made her voice go all deep and serious but I couldn't really understand why it was funny; my parents made fun of so many things. My earliest memories are all mixed up with the endless sunshine, the servants and the creatures that entertained me in my childhood world.

2

The bedroom I shared with John was next to a rubber hedge which separated our bungalow from the superintendent's mansion next door. The hedge squeaked and creaked in an alarming way when a storm was brewing. Sometimes the wind blew so strongly that it ripped whole branches off the hedge and spewed them on the ground. We picked them up and dipped our fingers in the sticky white sap that oozed out in order to test how well it made our fingers stick together. The sight of it made my mother shout. She frog-marched us into the kitchen and ordered us to wash our hands in the sink because she said the sap was poisonous. She said we'd go blind if we got it in our eyes. Lesley and Monique teased me that the creaking rubber hedge was really a wicked old witch whose knees squeaked when she sneaked around at night. They said the witch shut herself up in the wendy-house next to the rubber hedge and hid underneath the floorboards when daybreak came. John used to grind his teeth in his sleep and the sound of that and the creaking hedge made me lie awake at night. I dreamed that John ground his teeth so that they grew sharper than the witch's teeth. I listened to John's teeth and wound my sheet around my head. I prayed he'd manage to ward off the witch whose creaking joints matched the driving wind and the squeaking of the rubber hedge outside our window. Storms in the night have filled me with a terrible kind of unease all my life.

***

There was a flamboyant tree at the entrance to the driveway and its red flowers formed a thick carpet on the ground in the summer. The tree produced pods as big as boomerangs that fell around it in the winter. John and I threw them like helicopters across the lawn. We banged them against our hands so that the seeds inside them rattled like maracas. Eventually I got strong enough to break a pod over my knee so that we could line up the seeds and look at the wings they were beginning to sprout. They twirled through the air when the pods burst and the wind blew them like miniature spinning tops around the garden.

The sandy driveway provided us with an expanse along which we swept little roads with the sides of our feet. We created routes for our toy cars to race along and crash into each other around hair pin bends. The drive went up a gradual slope to the front door which was framed by a purple bougainvillea. In the summer it was festooned with sprays of flowers that vibrated with butterflies and wasps. I loved to pick the flowers and mix up medicines in an old tin mug. I made potions out of all the different kinds of flowers that my mother planted - violets, orange poppies, little white pansies, deep red verbena, yellow nasturtiums and pale blue forget-me-nots. I was convinced that if I got the combination right, I'd be able to fly with the birds and the butterflies that glided around the garden. The beds along the driveway and around the front lawn spilled their petals like confetti when ferocious gusts of wind heralded the arrival of a late afternoon thunderstorm. There was a rose garden over the way from the front door. Its pink, red and cream flowers littered the ground with sweet smelling petals all summer. It lay between the shelter and an old wall where Lesley spent hours hitting a tennis ball against it in the hot sun. An oil palm tree towered above the shelter and an ivy covered bird bath made of cement stood underneath in its cool shade. The palm tree looked like a giant umbrella that spewed great talons of leaves high up above its matted trunk. In its highest recesses nestled bunches of oily nuts that fell to the earth like yellow marbles after a torrential shower. John and I skidded about on their slippery skins as they lay rotting on the damp of the paving, and the air beyond wobbled in a wall of heat.

The little house had a corrugated iron roof which the men from the Public Works Department painted silver instead of red. My father spoke Afrikaans to the men who brought black men with them to do the work. John and I watched as they painted the outside walls of the house a chalky white. Our bedroom, with its swirling burglar bars, was painted a creamy yellow. The smell of the paint kept us awake at night until the hot air baked it dry the next day. At night the corrugated iron roof cracked and groaned as it cooled down. This frightened us until our mother told us that it was only the roof getting used to being out of the blistering sun.

My parents' bedroom looked out over the front garden. Below a pale blue window ledge was a cream and pink frangipani bush that attracted so many butterflies, wasps and bees that it resembled a railway station frequented by miniature passengers. On a still summer's day, its pungent scent drifted up into my parents' bedroom where it mingled with the smells of my father's aftershave and my mother's perfumes. 'Apple blossom', 'blue grass' and 'old spice' spring to mind and bring back the joy I felt when I lay between them while they read their newspapers, smoked their cigarettes and sipped the tea that was delivered by a servant carrying a big wooden tray. A sweet silence lay between us when the only sound was the rustling of the paper mixed with the tender feel of softening starch on their crumpled sheets.

An image of Monique hammering 'chopsticks' on the piano and me being danced around, with my feet on top of my father's feet, comes back. Lesley remembers our house being full of books and music and art and games. I remember how my father held me over the flower bed to do a wee and how I used to worry about it after my sisters teased me that a wasp or a bumble bee might mistake my bottom for a big white flower.

***

My granny in England sent Lesley a book about southern African butterflies to help her identify all the ones she killed and mounted in glass cases. My father got ether from the hospital so that she could kill the butterflies by dropping them, still flapping, into an old jam jar. Then she picked them out and mounted them on a sheet of cork board, using little paper strips to make their wings stretch out and stay flat. When our granny came to visit us in 1959, she took photos of Lesley's butterfly collection in the display cases on the wall. I remember how proud I felt when Lesley let me take her collection to school for a science exhibition.

Granny Alice brought lots of presents with her from England. She gave Lesley a little combustion engine that shunted along all by itself. My father got it going it with a flick of his cigarette lighter. Thin wisps of smoke unfurled from its funnel as it went across the room. She gave us a tinker toy set to share. It had a wooden hammer that we fought over. I remember the joy of making rockets, and diggers and motor cars out of red, green, blue and yellow sticks. Granny Alice gave me and Monique each a hug-a-bug. Mine was black and the one she gave Monique was white. I remember her blowing it up for me, until it turned itself into a squeaky black baby. Granny Alice said that my hug-a-bug was the same as the African piccanins that snuggled against their mothers' backs, tied on with blankets. My hug-a-bug had round arms and legs and I made it hang off me like a baby Kaola bear. It had a big open mouth and one of its eyes looked like it was winking. It had two hollow loops for ears and a painted curl on top of its forehead. I used to take it into the bath with me where I washed it with Lifebuoy soap, like my nanny Mary did when she washed me. I put the hug-a-bug on my lap so it could listen to the story about Little Black Sambo who was chased by some tigers around a tree. Little Black Sambo ran so fast round the tree that the tigers gradually melted into one another and turned into golden yellow butter. I sang songs to my hug-a-bug about Noddy and the Gollywog, and I spanked its bottom for being messy and dirty and splashing water out of the bath.

My granny also gave me a miniature Indian doll called Pocahontas. I loved its soft leather dress with tassels along the bottom. The doll had jet black hair tied back with a leather thong into a long pony tail. It wore a leather papoose on its back but there was no baby in it. The papoose didn't look nearly as warm and comfortable as the blanket that Mary wore to keep her baby snoozing on her back. She gave John a collection of Matchbox cars. I remember her buying John a doll at Haddon and Sly so that he had one like mine. Most of the photographs I have when John and I were very young were taken by our grandmother during her visit in 1959. After that Lesley became the official photographer in our family; my parents never owned a camera. The few photographs of us children together were portraits taken in a photographic studio when John was a cherubic one year old.

My memories of my grandmother include things like the milk shakes she made and the play dough she pummelled in the kitchen with my mother. John and I loved watching her make milkshakes for us with a hand whisk. She used food colouring to make 'green mambas', 'brown cows' and 'pink elephants'. When I think about my granny I remember a stout old woman, as round as our nannies, who wore her hair in a long grey plait. She wound the plait around and around her head so that it made an alice-band and a sort of hat at the same time. Lesley and Monique wore their hair in plaits in the photographs my granny took of them. My hair was cropped short so I got one of my sisters to make some grey wool into a long plait and I hung it over my head; its two ends swung underneath my sun hat and I twirled around like they did, watching my plaits flying along beside me.

***

I can't remember exactly when our grandmother visited us the second time and that's probably because she had had a serious stroke. Monique remembers visiting her in the Edith Duly Nursing Home where she stayed for quite a long time. Lesley said that she smelled of some special oil that she used to massage into her immobile arm. I remember my granny cradling her one arm in her other arm, and that her smile wasn't a proper smile any more. Nobody can remember exactly when our Granny Alice died. Lesley says she was working as a governess for an opera singer in La Jolla in America, when she had a second stroke and passed away.

Lesley wrote:

> *"My only memory of her death is that it happened when we were still living in the little house and that I wondered whether or not I felt sad because, I think, hers was the very first death that I had experienced. I remember thinking that I was supposed to feel sad when someone died and wondered whether what I was feeling was that."*

Her being in America would explain why I can't get hold of her death certificate.

My mother wrote:

> *"Mother probably died July or August 1964 – Penny took charge of funeral arrangements – Norman being unwilling to take time off from work to allow me to go to England – it was NOT a happy time in my life, nor in my marriage."*

3

My mother said that when John was around ten months old he caught pneumonia.

She wrote:

> "You were 20 months old when John was born.... I gave him very small amounts of "Farex" from age approx. three weeks – then he was happy and FULL – he began to sleep well. He, I wonder if you remember, was very ill with pneumonia when he was 10 months old – he was already walking – but still partially breast-fed. He was taken into the Mater Dei and abruptly weaned – in an oxygen tent – and literally, almost died. Neville Saunders found a new antibiotic – literally just introduced on the market – and tried it on this poor child, who remarkably, benefited from it, and made a very smooth recovery – although it was noticeable that he had suffered emotionally from being "snatched" into the Mater Dei and he was very "clingy" to me for some weeks – and I suspect his tendency to "dither" stems from that unsettled period in his early life. You probably suffered too – for all my focus at that time was on HIM and you were "of moment". You were well – healthy and Mary did a lot of looking after you when I was visiting John – perhaps that's what made you jealous of him – you were approx. two and a half years old and had never shown up to then, nor after so far as I know, any overt signs of jealousy. You never hit him, or pinched, bit or punched him – you just "bossed" him around."

Mary was our first nanny. She looked after me all the time that my mother had to go and be with John at the hospital, and then Mary looked after John when he came home again. She carried John around and sang him songs. Mary talked in a loud voice and when she smiled her teeth were so white and bright that I felt happy too. She smelled different to my mother because her smokiness was not the same as cigarettes. Mary cooked over a fire in her shack behind the garage. I used to sit inside it with her, and watched her dip her *sadza* into a black pot with brown stew in it. Mary heated up her iron kettle on the fire and gave me some of the bread she dipped into her tin mug. It tasted sweet and warm and tinny. I used to creep into that dark little room behind the garage when no one was there. There were no windows and it had a smooth dirt floor. It was like being in a cave until my eyes got used to being out of the sun and the floor was cool and pleasant on the soles of my bare feet. In the middle of the room was the open fire with its metal grid, and Mary's sleeping mat was against a wall at the back.

After Mary had her baby, she brought it with her to live in the shack for a while. The baby was fat and very black like Mary. It slept soundly on her back as she went about her chores around the house. Mary tied the baby onto her with an old blanket, so all you could see was its fuzzy little head lolling to one side as she bent over to pick John up or to sweep the floor. One day I crept into Mary's room and found her baby sitting by itself on the floor. The baby sat and stared at me with its big black eyes. I noticed snot streaming out of its nose, and that it didn't seem to mind the flies that buzzed in and out of the snot. I rushed over at the baby and gave it a giant push so it flew over backwards with a thud. I ran back into the house and hid underneath my eiderdown. My ears tingled as I lay there and listened to the baby screaming. I stayed where I was, long after the baby had stopped crying, until, eventually, Lesley or Monique found me. I remember how one of them sat on top of me and tickled me until the tears ran down my cheeks.

I look at the photographs of John with our nannies and I remember Mary and Margaret with a love that burns. Maybe my mother thought I was too big to need much cuddling and that's why she only employed one nanny at a time. Perhaps she just never gave it any thought at all.

John used to call me 'girlie' when he was just starting to talk, and he trailed around after me. One day I invited him to climb inside an old trunk in the garage and instructed him to lie down. I slammed the lid shut and sat on it while I put the padlock through an iron loop. One of the servants must have heard him shouting and let him out. Nobody punished me. I guess the servants never told anyone about it. They must have known that I'd have been in big trouble with my parents.

My mother told us how Mary smashed some vinyl LP records on her husband's head when he came home drunk one night. She described how Mary had picked up the nearest thing to hand, hit him with the records and shouted at him to 'basop' and leave. It may be that Mary left because her husband didn't listen to her. Lesley thought it was because Mary was no longer allowed to live at our house with her own child.

Margaret was our second nanny. She had lighter brown skin compared to Mary and, in the photos, she looks a good deal older than Mary. Margaret was joined by other servants and I remember Anderson, our cook, with a lot of fondness. He used to sit in the shade under the palm tree, holding his round mirror in one hand and combing his wiry hair into a wide parting down the middle of his head. He had a neat moustache like my father's. His white outfit looked like starched cardboard against his black skin. My mother taught him how to make Yorkshire puddings and roast beef. The only thing Anderson never learned to do was bake. My mother was a master chef when it came to making cakes and her chocolate cakes were the best. She made butter cream chocolate icing and decorated it with little silver balls. She whizzed a fork across the top of the icing and turned it into wavy patterns that reminded me of the sea. Perhaps the silver balls were there to serve as pearls of wisdom and a warning not to eat more than one piece of cake at a time.

Monique remembers Anderson's kindness to her:

> *"Don't know which was worse, being told by Mum that 'Dad will deal with you when he gets home' or Dad 'dealing with me!!!' Do you recall the time I went to the circus without permission – God, you would have thought the world ended. I got a 'hiding' and wasn't allowed to go anywhere for ages. But Anderson the cook at the time at Ingutsheni made up for it by making me a nice plate of sausages and tomato sauce to console me! I remember Dad once hit Lesley so hard he actually lifted her off her little feet!!! God knows what the poor little thing had done – she was always smaller than me – in my mind. I think he once told me it was good discipline but he didn't hit any of us once we got into our teens! Probably today he would be considered an abusive Father. I know that my friend's mother did give [her children] the odd smack. But nothing as violent as we had to go through. The strange part of it was it was mostly initiated by Mum. We certainly did have a strange childhood – wandering*

around the bush alone at very young ages – walking alone to see friends in Hillside – and the extremely strange belief that at five o'clock each day any friends who had come over had to go home and the house had to be perfect so when Dad came home all was 'perfect'."

It was Anderson who came to the rescue when one of us woke in the morning to see the black shape of a rain spider on the mosquito net. Anderson would be sent along with a broom stick to hit the rain spider off the net. I waited, shivering under my sheet, while he clubbed the spider to death on our floor. Rain spiders were commonplace in the summer months, when rain deluged our garden and turned it into a sweet smelling swamp.

A sudden thunderstorm brought instant relief from the blazing heat of the afternoon. It also made our servants rush outside in excitement. They used my mother's colander and sieve to scoop up squirming heaps of flying ants to add to the stews they cooked over their fire. They also roasted locusts and freshly picked mealies (sweet corn) over the open fire in the shack behind the garage. The smell of charred skin and the morsels John and I were given to eat are fond memories that linger still. It made no difference that we couldn't understand a word they were saying for they never shooed us away. I squatted on the floor next to them and I breathed in their smells along with the loudness of their chatter.

***

Our garden at the little house teemed with living things. Besides the flying ants there were praying mantises and the millipedes we called *chongololos*. Chongies were easy to catch because as soon as you touched them, they rolled themselves up into a coil. I used to put a rolled up chongie on my hand and sit on the front step, waiting patiently for it to unravel itself. It would gently uncurl itself and tickle its way up my arm with its hundreds of waving legs and then make its delicate way around the back of my neck. I used to chase the bulldog away from a chongie sleeping contentedly in the sun. It upset me if anything dented their hard outer shells because their blood was yellow and not red.

There were blue winged wasps whose stings were poisonous and ants that marched in long battalions from one end of the garden to the other. The ants formed lines of tiny sticks which moved in wriggling streams across the driveway. Margaret showed us how to scrape the muddy coating off a tree trunk and suck the sugary bits left behind by the white ants underneath. I loved to sit and watch army ants with their shiny black bodies and big pincers. John and I would put a stick into an army ant hole and wait for one of them to clamp itself on the end. There we would sit for long periods, mesmerised by the sight of the ant with its hard polished body writhing about on the end of a stick. John once stuck his finger in a hole. I remember how we looked in awe at the teeth marks on the end of his finger once he'd stopped crying.

We checked the muddy puddles for water scorpions before we splashed around in them. It was easy to mistake their black tails for twigs. There were certain scorpions whose stings were so painful and poisonous that they were deadly. I remember how I'd always look for a black shape at the bottom of a swimming pool, in case it was a water scorpion and not a leaf. I'd once seen 'a leaf' swim its way to the surface and so I always went and got the scoop to check before jumping into the water.

***

John had a brush with death one day in the Miller's swimming pool. He climbed down the ladder until he got to the bottom of the pool. I ran inside to get my mother. My mother couldn't swim and neither could I - so we stood on the side of the pool while Mrs Miller jumped in with her high-heels on and brought John back to the surface.

***

Our servants spent their time polishing, scrubbing, picking things in the vegetable garden, sweeping, watering, cleaning and cooking. Compared with our mother and father, they seemed to be life itself. Their bodies shook when they laughed and their hands slapped together when they said hello and goodbye. They sucked air in between their front teeth and made funny sounds when they talked. John copied Anderson when he shouted 'haikona' as a warning and when he went 'ugh ugh ugh' like a train chugging up a hill when something was wrong. They made that train noise when we got hurt.

Mary blew on John's knees when they were bleeding and I sat in the warmth of Margaret's lap when something upset me. She clicked her tongue, and said "shame shame" and "agh agh" until I stopped crying. John once got an enormous thorn in his foot and Margaret put his foot up to her mouth so that she could pull the thorn out with her teeth.

***

Margaret showed me how to trail a tiny stick around the rim of an ant-bear hole. It would not take long before an ant-bear shot itself upwards in a shower of sand, thinking that the stick was an ant. I spent hours trailing a twig around the perimeters of ant-bear holes, waiting in anticipation for the shock of a sudden attack. When an ant had the misfortune of being snared, I watched in fascination as it disappeared kicking and scrabbling into an early grave beneath the sand.

4

I can't recall when bulldogs first became part of our family life. The first dog was a stripy one named Tiger. He had to be returned to the farmer who'd bred him after he sank his teeth into Lesley's hand. Next was Hardy, the bulldog my mother named after Thomas Hardy. He was a big white dog with a brindle face and floppy wet jaws. The only bit of Hardy I used to stroke affectionately was his chin because it made him gaze at me with droopy eyes, while a contented little smile formed between his pointy bottom teeth.

One morning I was playing alone underneath the flamboyant tree. I'd found a healthy crop of ant-bear holes and was preoccupied with tempting some of them to make an attack. Hardy was lying dozing in the middle of the road, not far away. I saw Mr Radcliffe's silver jaguar coming down the road. I thought he would stop when he got closer to me and the dog lying in the road. But Mr Radcliffe drove straight over the sleeping bulldog, turned left, crossed the little bridge over the open sewer and was gone. In the clouds of dust he left behind, Hardy started howling in the most pitiful way, and I ran into the house to get my mother. I found her in the kitchen and she came running, with flour on her hands and her apron flying from her neck. She held the dog's head in her lap and I remember his poor old chin was all dotted with blood and dust and bits of sand. He squirmed about in her arms, making an awful whimpering noise. She sent me to go and tell Shadrick our 'house boy' to bring a sheet out of the cupboard. They wrapped the injured dog in it. Then Shadrick picked Hardy up and put him on the backseat of my mother's car. She drove off, leaving a trail of dust. I thought Hardy was going to die so I went and hid under my eiderdown. But, a few hours later, he came back home from the vets, alive and snuffling as usual.

Mr Radcliffe often came to drink whisky with my parents and patted me on the head when he saw me. He wore a dark blue suit with grey stripes on it. He had a pink handkerchief which peeped out of his top pocket and matched his pink tie. I remember him being much older than my parents and that he spoke with the same sort of accent as my mother. Mr Radcliffe didn't live in the grounds of

Ingutsheni like we did. I guess he didn't want to mix with the Afrikaners and Irish people who lived in the hospital grounds. My mother mentioned George Radcliffe in her diary. In an entry on 11th January 1980 she wrote: "*G. Radcliffe died, a brave, kind man – death is a kind relief.*"

Male nurses were given houses at Ingutsheni if they had a family to support. They lived in a compound over the road from the nurses' home. The female nurses and the matron lived in rooms inside the Nurses' Home which had a private tennis court to one side of it. The court was made of tarmac and sometimes John and I went and kicked a ball around on it. We were forbidden to go to the male nurses' houses because of the Finnegan's. My mother told us that Mrs Finnegan had invited her over for tea and that her children had a monkey tied to a tree in their backyard. She said the monkey screeched in a horrendous way and that she'd seen the children throwing rocks at it and tormenting it. When I was older one of the Finnegan boys invited me to his school dance. When he came to the door, I ran and hid underneath my bed. I made John go and tell him that I couldn't come with him because I had sunstroke.

The caretaker of the hospital grounds was Andreas Bezuidenhout. His house was on the corner of the dirt track that led to our house. The front of the Bezuidenhout's house was covered by a huge bougainvillea creeper and, when we drove past, I used to think of the Sleeping Beauty and the prince who chopped his way through thorns and branches to rescue the princess. My mother told us that Andreas' niece was a famous tennis player and that she'd played at Wimbledon.

On the other side of the road from Andreas' house lived the hospital clerk, a man my father called 'Bulldog' Drummond. Lesley and Monique went to the same school as the Drummond children and were sometimes invited to swim at their house. The pool was a round metal tank with steps up one side. So dense was the shade in that bit of their garden that the water inside the tank looked as black as ink. The Drummond's house was hidden away behind a ubiquitous rubber hedge whose rubbery fingers made it impossible to see.

Sometimes my mother drove us up to my father's office and we caught sight of European men playing bowls in their striped pyjamas on a bowling green as flat as cardboard near the administration block. She wouldn't take us with her into the office block, so John and I sat in the car and bickered in the sweltering heat. My father's office was nearest the wood panelled door at the front. I could see an enormous wooden fan whirling around on the ceiling of his office as we waited for our mother to come out to the car and take us home.

***

My parents didn't socialise with any of the people who lived at Ingutsheni. My mother became close friends with Winifred Davies who was the occupational therapist at the hospital. Winifred used to drop by our house after work. She and my parents would sit outdoors underneath the thatched shelter and smoke their cigarettes. We children played nearby while the servants came and went with pots of tea or glasses chinking with ice cubes. In the winter, when they sat in the lounge, we were invited in to say "Hallo". I stood at the door and watched my mother use a pair of silver tongs to pluck ice out of a silver bucket. She dropped ice cubes into their drinks with a crack while their cigarettes made smoky trails around their heads. She would hand us over to Mary or Margaret to be taken off for a bath and then put to bed. Winifred, with her blonde bob and pointy shoes, had a clipped way of speaking and a shrieky laugh. She didn't have a deep voice like my mother nor did she have my mother's musical way of petting the bulldog that came and snuffled under her skirt.

Years later, when I was expecting my first child, I got in touch with Winifred. She sent me a cassette recording of her memories of working at Ingutsheni. She described how she'd decided to apply for the job in Rhodesia after a pea soup fog stopped all the buses on her way to work one freezing morning in London. She departed for Africa and started work at Ingutsheni in 1953. She said, on her first day, she was shown into a dormitory with a small table stuck down between the beds and two green cupboards at the end where she thought the patients kept their clothes; there was one broken loo and one broken pair of scissors and that was the sum total of what she had to start with. She decided she could teach the patients to sew, paint, play the odd game, get their hair cut, and eventually she did a lot of dress making with them. She said she found it all very tricky to start with. She used to take some of the patients on early morning walks in the orange groves and along a jacaranda avenue to the far end of the hospital grounds. She taught them to play grandmother's footsteps and introduced ball games to a mixture of people who ranged in age from seventy to ten year olds. Winifred said that, in the early days of her time at Ingutsheni, children as young as eight were kept in with the adults. When the St. Francis Home for Mentally Handicapped Children was built in 1957, that problem was solved.

She said the patients' diet was appalling. They lived on mince with *sadza* (mealie meal) served on tin plates. There were no vegetables and always rice pudding for desert. I suspect that the European patients' diet was a bit better because many of them had visits from relatives.

Winifred said that ECT (electro-convulsive therapy or 'shock treatment') was widely used, with quite a heavy use of drugs, because in those days it was before the advent of the Chlorpromazines and things – they were only just coming in, and their use wasn't as wide spread as it is now. She said, with hindsight, that it would have been possible to perhaps have done more, to have done a bit of counselling – the skills which she developed much later in her life when she went to St. Bartholomew's Hospital in London, and headed their academic unit of psychiatry there, where it was nearly all counselling. However, she said, that wasn't to be at Ingutsheni.

Winifred said she'd been involved in the design and building of the new women's ward and its outdoor exercise yard with the iron flamingos I remember so clearly. She said there was great excitement when the time came to move out of the little bungalow-type place where she started work, and into the new building. They had some decent tables on which they could cut out fabrics or do some painting. They got some old comfy chairs and painted them different colours. Winifred said she had the girls make some rugs, so that in front of the fire place they had a rug to make it look homely. She got a treadle sewing machine and then a typewriter on which she taught some of the patients to touch type. Eventually she got a radio gram and a gramophone and, with some money and donated records and tokens, she got quite a good collection of music. It was in the days of Elvis just becoming well known. Winifred said the whole building was a locked unit. So, apart from escaping through the bars, or somehow, it was a lot more spacious but it was also more confined. But, because of the arrangement of the courtyards and the sort of iron grill work – which was very prettily done – there was much more air and there was a feeling of being more part of the outside world.

Winifred remembered three Polish women who were admitted to Ingutsheni. She said they were 'very mad and their English non-existent'. She felt desperately sad for these ladies because they were refugees. She said that during the latter end of the war, the women had been shuffled all the way down from Poland, through the Middle East and down to Africa. She had no idea what had happened to them to produce such cataclysmic results in their mental condition. She said there were other patients who cried and clung around her ankles saying 'help, help'. A suggestion to teach the African women to throw traditional pots was beyond her remit, she said. Male patients were taught to make furniture and mattresses by a man called Dawie Kok.

Winifred spoke of the riots that began in the latter part of 1961. She remembered how her car got stoned by a mob as she was trying to get into the gates of Ingutsheni. She had to run the gauntlet and said how grateful she was that the African warders came to her rescue. They cheered her on and shouted "Come on madam, come on madam" – so she got safely into the hospital grounds. The police wouldn't let her leave without an escort, and one of the men came home with her that night in the car. She said there were other nights when there was rampaging in the African locations so she went and stayed with friends.

***

Winifred fell in love with an American citizen and eventually emigrated to the USA towards the end of 1962. During the process of applying for an American visa, Winifred said my father helped her warn off a consular official who attempted to rape her. She'd had to lock her front door while this man remained on the other side, berating her and doing his best to break into her flat.

***

I still have the antique bracelet that Winifred gave my mother when she left for America. It has a moonstone set in the middle of a delicate gold coil. My mother said the bracelet was made of 18 carat gold and worth a bob or two. I think Winfred must have picked it up at an auction. She and my mother used to go together to bid for rugs and antique furniture from England. I inherited some of my mother's china plates, with marks on the back that say: Spode, Coalport and Minton. In the photographs I have of the interiors of the various houses we lived in, my mother's flair for choosing mahogany and oak relics from England, and colourful oriental rugs from Persia, created an opulent background to my African childhood.

5

I look at a photograph of me in my white party dress. I see the wide bow tied tightly behind my back and my new white shoes. Behind me I see the garden tap and the paved pool where the water collected. I remember how the servants went to and fro in the sweltering heat with their watering cans, slopping water as they tended to the abundant flowers and the vegetable garden. I look at the arum lilies near the tap that John ate when he was pretending to be Chicken Licken, and I remember how my mother rushed him to hospital when he couldn't stop throwing up. A chilly memory grips me like the time John nearly died of pneumonia. The same excruciating feeling comes over me as I gaze at the photo. I remember that I broke a sugar bowl at that party and never attended another, nor was allowed a party myself. The party was for the superintendent at Ingutsheni, not long before he retired. I guess my father was hoping that he would be the next in line for the top job, and my careless behaviour got mixed up with his failure. I look at another photograph of me in my party dress that afternoon. This time I'm sitting arm in arm with John, and we're laughing into the camera. In many photographs, John sits or stands beaming next to me, with his angelic face and chubby good looks. He was a beautiful little boy.

***

The annual hospital fete was held at the St. Francis Home for Mentally Handicapped Children. We got into the car with my parents and they drove past the women's ward and up the avenue of jacarandas to the Home. The road was like a sheet of corrugated iron in the summer months and the car juddered its way over the ruts until we reached the gleaming white walls of St. Francis.

Mother Alana was the Mother Superior at St. Francis. Her beaming face peeped out from her stiff white head dress when she stepped out of the front door to greet us. She didn't seem to mind how it squeezed her chin and made her skin crinkle. She spoke in a soft Irish whisper and did a little curtsy when my father, and then my mother, shook her hand. Her head dress made it difficult for her to look down at me but I noticed that she had dimples that went in and out of her cheeks when she talked. She wore a long necklace with a shiny silver cross at the bottom. It swayed in a rhythmic way when she walked along next to us and her skirt rustled as she led us around the Home to see the children. Her shoes squeaked along the shiny black corridors and I remember a sugary smell that leaked out of the silent rooms and down the empty passages.

I didn't like looking at the children and babies in their cots. None of them could speak. Their faces were all twisted and some of them dribbled or had white foamy stuff between their lips. On one of those visits, a girl about the same age as me came and held on to my skirt. When I protested and tried to push her away, Mother Alana had to call one of the nuns to come and release the girl's fingers from my dress. The girl wouldn't let go and two nuns came and dragged her away. The girl let out a scream that echoed down the corridors as they carted her off. She ripped a hole in my pink net petticoat and I began to cry. Mother Alana leaned down and smiled her dimpled smile as she straightened up my skirt. Then she gave me her handkerchief to dry my eyes. I remember it was embroidered with pale blue forget-me-nots.

On those visits, John and I couldn't wait to get out of the wards and into the open air. At one of the fetes my mother bought me a Humpty Dumpty that had been knitted by hand. She said the people at Toc H were very good at knitting. My Humpty Dumpty wore a stripy jumper but his arms and legs were too long and spindly for him to stand on his own. He had a black top hat stitched on the side of his head like a chimney. I remember taking Humpty Dumpty on the tractor with me for the ride up to the hospital farm. We climbed into a big iron trailer behind the farm tractor and an African in blue overalls gunned the engine. John once burned the backs of his knees on the seat because the trailer had been standing in the sun. He stopped crying when a nun gave him a pink candyfloss on the end of a stick.

The tractor bumped us down the jacaranda avenue, around all the hospital buildings, and crunched its way down a black cinder track until the open fields of the hospital farm came into view. We weren't allowed to go into the fields where rows of strawberries and mealies and potatoes stretched away into the distance. I remember how the air above the crops wobbled in the heat and iron sprinklers sputtered shots of water that wafted over to where we were playing. I loved how the boiling earth smelled of warmth and food and growth whenever a sprinkler swept its way past us. We were told to keep out of the spray. We played in the empty barns in amongst the hay bales until someone blew a whistle and we rattled our way back to the Home. My mother greeted us with sticks of pink candy floss. We squeezed chunks of it into dark pink balls between our muddy fingers and swallowed it in wiry clumps.

When we got home, John and I sat on the black granolith step and stuck our tongues out at each other to see whose had been dyed the most luminous pink. The smooth black granolith stayed warm long after the sun sank and stopped heating it to boiling point. As the last rays slanted across the garden, it was soothing to sit there and wait for night to fall. Night apes spied down on us from the eaves of the house, crickets and frogs set up their night time choruses and fire flies danced above the old iron bucket next to the garden tap. When the red sun slipped away beneath the trees, night fell like a power cut for there were no street lights at Ingutsheni. There were no street names, no passing cars, no shops and no neighbours, save for our servants in their shack behind the garage and the screaming inmates over the way.

***

Lesley and Monique teased us that Father Christmas wouldn't come all the way from the North Pole to visit us at Ingutsheni. They said it was far too hot for him and anyway the chimney at the little house was blocked up. They said that, without a decent chimney, Father Christmas wouldn't be able to sneak in like he did in England. They laughed and said that Father Christmas might mistake the iron chimney in the servants' shack for ours. I cried and shouted that my father would catch the servants and smack them if they ran off with my presents.

6

My father's office was so close by that he came home every day for lunch. One day he came home to find me chasing butterflies with Lesley's butterfly net when I was supposed to be at the Little People's Nursery School. He spanked me hard and said that if I was sick then I needed to be in bed. He locked me in my bedroom saying that if I was too sick for school, then I was too sick for lunch.

On another occasion, while my mother was unloading her shopping from the car, I pushed John onto the hand brake and the car rolled down the drive. My mother dropped her shopping and ran next to the car, her anxious face looking at us through the side window, until she managed to pull the door open and climb inside. She pulled up the handbrake before the car could roll out of our driveway and into the smelly sewer over the road. When my father came home that evening he gave us each a hiding. He shouted at us for giving our mother such a fright and sent us to bed without any supper.

***

One night I was woken up by sharp flashes of lightning. It was pitch black in our room. I lay in bed and watched the room light up as if someone was flicking a switch on and off. So bright was each flash that I could clearly see the big wooden fan on the ceiling above me. Then I heard another sound which made my heart start to race. It was the sound of John cracking and grinding his teeth. Another flash of lightning was followed by a forceful gust of wind that made the rubber hedge creak in a meaningful way. An ear tingling crackle of lightning meant that a gigantic crash of thunder was about to split the heavens. I scrambled out of bed and raced down the dark passage to my parents' bedroom. A clap of thunder like a volcanic explosion made the hairs on the back of my neck stand on end. John started to wail and so did I.

My father was already out of bed. He snatched me up and stumbled with me under one arm back to our room. His heavy nasal breathing and the smell of his bryl-creamed hair made me squirm and I tried to run back to my mother. He threw me onto my bed and

34

another flash of lightning lit up his face. I saw his grey hair all wild on the top of his head and he didn't look like my father any more. I screamed and he smacked me so hard that I bounced off the bed and hit my head on the wall. He carried on hitting me. He said I was to stop making such a bladdy noise or I would wake up the entire hospital. Then he stumbled off to bed.

Lightning continued to strobe the room. Thunder exploded and boomed with such violence that the bars on the windows jangled. I looked over at John's bed and saw that he was gone. In that moment I knew that my mother had followed along behind my father and taken John back to bed with her. I lay like a small statue and waited while the rain battered the iron roof and drowned out every other sound. Eventually, some frogs started to sing and their raucous voices filled the darkness with a strangely calming noise. After that, when thunder and lightning bombarded our bedroom and the rain drummed on the roof, as soon as the frogs' chorus began, I knew that it was safe for me to stop holding my breath. As their croaky voices grew in number I would gradually relax and fall asleep.

When a storm brewed in the daytime, my mother would point out the anvil-shaped clouds that grew as the sun heated up the earth and the sky disappeared. A sudden silence grew as the cicadas stopped their ringing songs and flew off to find cover. She said God had an enormous workshop in the sky and the clouds were made from the billows he used to stoke up His fire; that's what made the sun stop shining behind the grey clouds. She said that the lightning was God's flashlight that he used to find his way home. It crackled and flashed because he was always short of batteries, so God did a lot of grumbling as he rode along on his bicycle. She said it was hard for God to ride his bike through all the billowing clouds because they grew so thick and so black. She said the thunder was the sound of God shouting when He fell off his bike. The rumbling thunder was him mumbling bad words to himself when he got back on the bike and went on his way.

7

The Boschoffs invited us to Cape Town for a holiday towards the end of 1959. We were taken to the station in the hospital bus called 'the safari'. The shopping district next to the station buzzed with Africans milling about, the women wearing brightly coloured head scarves (doeks) and the men standing in groups, smoking cigarettes and chatting. Women carried baskets, and fruit, and laundry on their heads and babies hung dozing on their backs, their heads wobbling from side to side as they walked along talking and gesticulating with their friends.

My father was delighted to have a chance to show my mother his native city. The excitement of that trip is still palpable nearly sixty years later. The sight of the train, waiting patiently, smoke hissing out of the engine, sent me and John into a delirium of excitement. Lesley and Monique disappeared inside the carriage and we had to be helped up the iron steps. Inside our compartment we patted the green leather seats and admired the polished wooden panels. The train eventually pulled slowly out of the station with huge bursts of smoke. We stood in the corridor and watched the cars and people slowly give way to grassland and thorn trees. With the train firmly on its way, John and I arranged the green leather bolsters from the seats along the corridor next to our cabin. The bolsters made an obstacle course for us to jump over. John and I hurtled up and down, oblivious to the motion of the carriage as it clattered its way through the countryside. I remember how wonderful it was for me and John to sleep in the same compartment as our parents, while Lesley and Monique shared a smaller one next door. We felt very privileged.

The train pulled wearily to a stop at Mafeking in Bechuanaland and a gaggle of Africans ran alongside. They were ragged people with woolly hair and bare feet. There were women with old cloths wrapped around their heads and babies tied on their backs with towels and blankets. They called up to us as we stood peering down at them. Black hands held up carvings of African animals and spears and three-legged stools. Women held up crocheted table cloths and place settings. Boys pushed along toys made out of wire and wood with wheels made out of bottle tops and other rubbish. Girls waved necklaces and bangles made out of bright red lucky beans and tiny glass beads. Eyes pleaded, mouths were solemn, and flies drifted like clouds around every dusty person. The flies flitted onto trails of snot around noses and made sorties into upturned eyes; they buzzed around woolly heads and settled on lips and hands and feet. My mother bought a creamy table cloth and a wooden lion for me. Its mane was made from fur and its tail was blackened by fire. Years later it still smelled of wood smoke and something dead. Monique chose a tortoise carved out of dark wood. Its little head had two white dots for eyes and its shell was covered in intricate patterns. Lesley got a lucky bean necklace and John a beautifully carved wooden spear that he still owns.

The whistle blew and the crowd below pressed in closer and waved things more frantically. Final cries and pleading hands went up all over the little sea of natives as the train started to make its slow departure from Mafeking. We hung out of the window, watching them give chase until, finally, the train picked up speed and they were left far behind. My father wasn't interested in the bedlam outside the train and we ran off to show him our purchases in the dining car where he sat smoking and reading a newspaper. I remember Monique let me hold her wooden tortoise in exchange for my lion and I traced the patterns on its back with my tongue. My father snatched it away and yelled "agh siss man Cait". He said I'd catch some 'bladdy kaffir disease if I wasn't careful'.

My mother opened the window in the cabin just enough so the smuts wouldn't stick like miniature lead bullets in our eyelashes or spatter on top of our lovely white bedding. The engine's huffing and puffing echoed across the Karoo desert while the wheels clattered along in a sing-song rhythm. At meal times we followed our parents into the dining car, where the tables were set with big silver knives and forks and gravy dishes. My parents shook out the thickly starched napkins and stuffed them down our fronts. African waiters swayed rhythmically with the motion of the train and served us our food, their white uniforms as starched as the tableware. They used forks and spoons like tongs to deliver vegetables onto our plates.

The train whistled through the days and nights of our journey. We slept under crisp white sheets in bunks, one on top of the other. My father and John slept on the bottom. The top bunk allowed me to lie on my stomach and peer into the darkness through the shutters which made the cabin as dark as a cupboard. I woke up every time the train slowed to halt at a station along the way. Then I waited in eager anticipation for the train to start moving again. It moved so slowly at first that the only way to tell was to look at something like a rooftop or a tree to see whether it was us moving or a train gliding off alongside us. It caused a strange sensation inside my head, as if my body was being left behind. The same thing happened when the train came into a station. It seemed to take forever for it to slow down to a complete stop. My mother said it gave her the kittens if I put my head too far out of the window to try to see the platform. She gripped my skirt in case I fell out. I woke up on the last morning of our journey to look in amazement out of the window at vineyards and mountains. It felt as if we'd had arrived in an enchanted land.

We stayed with the Boschoff's for a few days. Mr. Boschoff sat me on his knee and nuzzled me with his beaky nose; I didn't like his yellow teeth or the smelly pipe he clamped between them when he talked. He sang "K-K-K-Katie" to me and "eeny weeny itsy bitsy polka dot bikini" to Lesley and Monique. The Boschoff's drove us to the Steenbrass Dam one day. Mrs Boschoff sang "She'll be coming round the mountain when she comes". I wanted to be sick because they'd taken us up Table Mountain the day before and the cable car had terrified me. There was something about the inky black water below us that filled me with anxiety. Looking back, I see how I must have associated that colour with the ink in my first fountain pen as I struggled to form my letters. I drew ships with angular bodies and smoking funnels like the ones I'd seen from the top of Table Mountain, drifting far below me. They were miniaturised hulks that left tiny plumes of smoke floating across the wide ocean that stretched like a blue desert as far as the eye could see. I loved to draw horses' heads from a sideways view, and gave them abundant fringes and eye lashes like the models I saw in my mother's magazines.

The Boschoffs lent us their car for a few days and we drove to Gordon's Bay. We stayed at the van Riebeck Hotel where the water from the Indian Ocean was calm and warm. Lesley remembers that my father played ping-pong endlessly with her and Monique, while

John and I went to the toy shop with my mother to buy buckets and spades and sweets. There was a flat sandy beach over the road from the hotel. I remember floating on my lilo, watching crabs scuttling around in the crystal clear water underneath me. The gentle shallows had a soothing effect that made the first few days drift along in a peaceful way.

Monique said that one morning Lesley floated a long way off on her lilo. She said my father shouted after Lesley and then ran in a frenzy a long way out over the water to get her. After that I became afraid of the crabs because they churned up the sand behind them in the same way my father's feet had done as he raced through the shallow water past me. My mother said she didn't know what they would have done if Lesley had drifted any further out because neither she nor my father could swim. After that I refused to get on my lilo in case it sailed me out to sea.

During the train journey back to Bulawayo I had a fight with my father over breakfast. I didn't like the eggs and fried tomato he ordered because the toast had gone all soggy and it made me gag. Nothing would persuade me to eat it. In our compartment that night I heard my father say that I was 'a bladdy pest'. He said he hadn't wanted to have any more children, that it was my mother's idea not his. The next morning, I watched him as he snipped his moustache in the mirror. He winked at me sitting behind him, but all I can remember is looking at the pointy tips of his scissors. The train had lost its music as it thundered its way back home.

8

Towards the end of 1960 we moved into the superintendent's house next door. The new superintendent didn't want his family to live at the hospital, and so Norman was given the house. It was clear from the first letter my father wrote me that he had felt overlooked for the top job.

He wrote:

"I have never regretted taking up Medicine and later Psychiatry. I enjoy people and found endless pleasure in helping people and also getting to know about people. I think although I say it myself that I was a good psychiatrist who would listen and was also well liked. My only medical problem while in Rhodesia was my colleague Dr Hamilton who took advantage of a few months seniority to me in the Rhodesian Mental Health Service and tended to make life rather difficult.

I think I was a good father to you and the others and was always very conscious of my need to give as much time as my work allowed to you. I have always had a great regard and respect for Elspeth's opinion and because of this encouraged her to take much more part in all your lives than perhaps other fathers did."

***

One evening, as John and I pushed our cars up and down the new dusty driveway, we drew near to our old home. We heard a boy singing "Figaro" over and over. Here was a sound that I could copy without Lesley or anyone else yelling at me to stop. John and I scampered back up to the house. John cupped his stubby hands around his mouth and we sang "Figaro, Figaro, Figaro" as loudly as we could. Our voices carried over the silver corrugated roof of the big house, above its twirling Dutch gables edged in powder blue, out into the bush towards Bulawayo and up into the Heavens. The shrieking inmates over the road were gone.

My mother wrote:

"The Wrights were first in the little house after the superintendent retired and we moved into the Big House. They built the pool. Their children (two girls) were teenagers and we were not all that socially

involved. Lesley and Monique went to senior school with them –
Mrs Wright taught science there. Lesley used to call Dr Wright
"Little Napoleon"!! She found him very dictatorial – I think!"

***

My father was wrinkled and generally lacking in muscles compared to Mohamed Ali and the all-in wrestlers that I loved to watch on television. It made John and I laugh one Guy Fawkes' night that he had to sprint for cover when a rocket he'd lit fell out of its bottle and pointed itself straight at him. We'd never seen my father lift a finger around the house, let alone run off like a frightened rabbit. We knew better than to laugh when it happened but, for months afterwards, the word 'rocket' made us collapse in hysterics.

It's strange to think of my father as a white person. He talked about 'rooi neks' (red necks) - a South African euphemism for English people – and yet he tanned himself as red as an old peach from head to foot every weekend. When the sky was grey, the house was filled with gloom when he sat in the lounge wearing his herringbone slacks and pure wool jumper. How I longed for the sun to shine, when he came in for lunch, bright red and smiling and stinking of Sea and Ski sun lotion. All my memories of him are lit by the sunshine that gave him his recreation, lying on his squeaky recliner and twiddling the knobs on his portable radio to get the latest cricket scores. I remember how the signature tune for the BBC Overseas Service wafted through the hot air, while white butterflies drifted over the flowerbeds like tails on an invisible kite. The grey hairs on his chest glittered with little bobbles of moisture and the wrinkles guttering his stomach made sweat leak out of them when he sat up in order to fit a cigarette into its holder. He huffed and puffed as he sat there gagging for a smoke and dribbling sweat all over the place. He's always sitting outside in my memories, his eyes hidden by his tear-drop dark glasses and his nose as red as a beacon.

I look at a photograph of my parents on a typical weekend afternoon. My mother, in her sleeveless cotton dress, stands next to my father sitting on his recliner, both with their cigarettes in their hands, and he with his skinny legs sticking out of his swimming trunks. She's wearing her gold sandals with her painted toe nails peeking out of them. I remember even on those sweltering afternoons she wore cloudy stockings that made her legs all silky and smooth. I remember how her pink toe nails were shrouded inside them and the seams up the backs of her legs looked as if someone had neatly stitched her together. There was only room for one person to sit on the recliner when my mother took out the tray of tea things, so she stood by idly chatting and puffing on her cigarette. He sat and sweated while they talked and sipped their drinks. He looks like a headman billowing smoke signals and she like the Queen Mother at a garden party, her blue-grey hair swept back on either side of her head. There were no servants around on the weekends so that's why my mother was on duty. The house was eerily silent, especially in the kitchen and on the back lawn compared to week days when the servants sat on an old sheet, shelling peas, peeling potatoes, polishing the silver, and chatting in a language I never understood.

I remember the atmosphere around my parents was quiet and secret on those weekend afternoons. I spent a life time straining my ears, hoping to hear my name alongside Lesley and Monique and John's. Little snatches of conversation would drift over to me sitting high up in a tree on the other side of the lawn while they chatted. "Ja …. Hell …" I heard my father laugh in between my mother's mumblings. I would eventually creep down from the branch I'd been sitting on, to land neatly in the cool shadow beneath the tree. I'd pick up my discarded butterfly net and be off on a chase through the bush in pursuit of my quarry, oblivious of the hot sand burning under my bare feet as I chased through the singing grass.

***

The hospital and its grounds became an expansive world for me to explore, first on foot, and then on my bicycle. Memories unfurl and I remember the time that my father had all his teeth out and came home with a plastic smile.

9

The superintendent's house, like the administration block where my father had his office, had a stone relief of a Zimbabwe bird embossed above the front door. The bird's ubiquitous image was on our coins, paper money, the Rhodesian flag, and it adorned the covers of guide books, pamphlets, history books and lots of other things.

The entrance hall oozed with alcoholic smells. Boozy odours seeped out of a carved wooden wine cooler next to the front door. My father's study near the front door served as the television room. It was my refuge after supper, situated as it was opposite the dining room. There I spent most evenings watching whatever was on. I watched Mohammed Ali, Sugar Ray Leonard and all-in wrestlers with peroxided hair and strange swimming costumes throwing each other out of an elasticated boxing ring. I watched the Cartwright brothers riding gallantly out of the blazing map of their Ponderosa ranch at the beginning of Bonanza. I sat captivated by the wagons that rolled along through thunderstorms in Rawhide and I fell in love with the Lone Ranger and Tonto. I laughed at the stupid American soldiers in F Troop and the even stupider Red Indians called the "Hekarwees" The Hekarwees were so named for saying "where the heck are we" because they were so stupid. The 'Red Skins' in the westerns that I loved were gunned down in their shrieking masses, while the American cowboys lasso-ed horses and cows and women without so much as a cut or a bruise on their manly bodies.

I loved American comedies like The Flying Nun, Hogan's Heroes, the Beverley Hill Billies, the Addams Family, and sitcoms like Bewitched, the Mary Tyler Moore Show, Phyllis Diller, Red Skelton, Bob Hope, The Benny Hill Show and I Love Lucy. Then there were English shows like Muffin the Mule, Sooty and Sweep, and Dr Who. I adored Mr Spock and James T. Kirk in Star Trek as they sailed around the universe in the spaceship Enterprise 'to boldly go where no man had been before'.

Every year I sat up all night watching the Mayor's Christmas Cheer Show and I never missed Top of the Pops. The unfolding story of The Fugitive, starring David Janssen as Dr Richard Kimble, a man on the run after being accused of murdering his wife, was an essential part of my viewing. The fact that justice eluded Dr Kimble without fail every week had me on the edge of my seat. I watched Alfred Hitchcock's film Psycho one night and crept back to bed, past my father's shower cubicle, where the cat had left muddy footprints on the floor. For a spine tingling moment I heard the horrible music from the shower scene and scuttled off to bed.

Whenever I watched the Mod Squad, and Clarence Williams III was on the screen, my father would laugh and say "There's that enigmatic kaffir! Good old enigmatic!" I never thought twice about the fact that our servants had English names, or were given names like "Innocent" or "Tuppence" or "Poison". The Africans I knew at Ingutsheni had no surnames. The word "kaffir" was an Arabic word to describe an "unbeliever" or "non-muslim" and it was used by Arab slavers who bought and sold the indigenous black people of Africa during the slave trade. Clarence Williams III was the first and only well-educated African I saw - on television.

***

I listened to Wrex Tarr and his comedy sketches. Tarr became a popular comedian, having started out as a news reader for the Rhodesian Broadcasting Corporation. He made two successful LP records called "Futi Chilapalapa" and "The Cream of Chilapalapa" in which he made fun of how Africans spoke English. He used a language which was known as "kitchen kaffir" or "chilapalapa". This language was also known as "fanakalo". It was derived mostly from IsiZulu and it included bits of English, Afrikaans and ChiShona words. The prefix "chi" signfies the speaker of a particular African dialect, and the word "lapa" means "here" in isiNdebele.

10

Servants vacuumed our bedrooms and polished the floors every morning. They laid the table every day with starched linen and shined our silver serviette rings, each engraved with our initials with Silvo polish. Starched napkins were washed and ironed in the hospital laundry at the end of every week.

On Christmas Day gold edged china was taken out of the oak dresser in the dining room. A trolley waited obediently next to the door into the kitchen, for the servants to wheel the courses in and out. While my father did his rounds in the wards in the morning, my mother put a silver bowl on the mantelpiece. She filled it with roses and flowers from the garden. She stuck bits of tinsel and silver baubles in amongst flowers in Christmas tones of red and orange and cream. We sat in the lounge and waited for hours, while my father went around Ingutsheni and delivered Christmas cards to the hospital staff. When he came in, my mother poured them each a drink out of a crystal decanter and they sat and sipped their drinks next to the Christmas tree. She fixed their cigarettes into holders and my father got his old lighter out of its leather case. She cupped her hand around his, lit both cigarettes and handed one to him. The smoke hung in little clouds above their heads while we sat patiently and eyed our presents. When my father was comfortably seated and sucking on his cigarette we were finally allowed to unwrap our presents. Lesley was given the signal to dish them out and the bulldog waddled from person to person, drooling hopefully for something to eat. As the present opening came to an end, my mother went into the kitchen to chivvy along the servants. The servants were given extra rations for staying on to polish the silver, do the cooking, serve the meal and wash up afterwards. A bell summoned us to the dining room where we pulled our crackers. My father's sunburnt face shone brightly underneath his paper crown.

***

Our spacious lounge had an enormous veranda off it. The veranda boasted three pairs of columns underneath a couple of graceful arches, adorned with curly Dutch gables. The black granolith floor made a slippery skating rink for me and John when we got home from school. Our white socks turned black as we raced along it and skidded into one another. A glass-topped wicker table and cushioned benches were there for us to sit on and sip our cool drinks, as we looked out over the terraced grounds of the garden towards Bulawayo in the distance. We could gaze over the bush, where the buzz of cars and heavy goods vehicles made their way along 23rd Avenue to the industrial sites nearby. The hospital's location gave the road a certain notoriety; naughty children were warned they'd go to "23rd Avenue" if they didn't behave themselves properly.

John and I shared a bedroom divided into two. I had the inner half, and John slept in the veranda bit. Lesley's room was next door, the same configuration as ours, with the bit that made up my bedroom serving as her storage area and dressing room. The windows to our bedroom had no burglar bars so we climbed in and out of it, without having to use the door to the garden which was in Lesley's room. I used to sneak into John's room after lights out. We would crouch near the key hole into Lesley's bedroom to catch the Lourenco Marques hit parade that she listened to on Friday nights.

Monique had the end bedroom which looked out over the front garden and our parents were sandwiched between her and us. The bedrooms were connected by a long narrow passage. Reminiscent of our train journey to Cape Town, John and I pushed the rug in the middle of it into humps and spent hours jumping over them. Monique was given a turntable for her birthday and suddenly the house was alive with pop music. I remember dancing to Eight Days a Week with my mother in the kitchen. Bridge over Troubled Water will always transport me to Monique's twenty-first birthday when John and I hid in the garden and spied on her dancing with her boyfriend Jamie on the top lawn in the moonlight.

A new shelter was built along one side of the garden that was bordered off from the surrounding bush by a familiar squeaking rubber hedge. The house was very grand compared to the bungalow we had left behind. My mother had a pantry and there was a porch next to the kitchen where the dog snored and snapped at flies in a giant wicker basket. The kitchen was big enough for a large rectangular table in the middle, where the servants prepared our food and on which I often sat listening to their chatter.

The drive up to the house was lined with Spathodia trees, known in Rhodesia as 'flame trees'. They produced huge plumes of burnt orange flowers in the summer - but it was the buds that John and I collected and stuffed into our pockets. The buds were covered in thick hairs and were shaped like crescent moons. On being sharply squeezed, a thick syrup squirted out and drenched an opponent with slime. The buds eventually burst their hairy skins to produce those fiery flowers. Their massed ranks, together with red poinsettias and hibiscuses, made the journey up to the big house stunningly beautiful in the summer. The drive swept around a circular fishpond adjacent to the front door and provided Monique's many boyfriends with an opportunity to perform wheel spins when they arrived to take her out. Jamie, I remember, called my mother 'the mother superior'.

The fishpond at the top of the drive was hidden underneath a half dome that had an ugly rockery cemented onto its back. Inside the dome water dribbled into the pond. Pink water lilies covered the surface under which large gold fish and energetic frogs swam, often leaping out of the water to snap at dragonflies that skimmed overhead. The bulldog would lie next to the pond, watching the fish and frogs as they glided in and out from under the lily pads. Sometimes he would pounce, his jowls flopping in the water. Then he would heave mouthfuls of water and plants onto the side, hoping to catch a fish or a frog. John and I fed the fish lumps of bread and caught them in the kitchen sieve. The sight of bits of bread and multitudes of fish nipping and fighting for food proved irresistible, and the dog would leap into the pond with a splash that frightened everything away into the murky depths of the pond for the rest of the day.

John and I used to sit at the water's edge waiting for a hideous toad that lived at the bottom of the pond to come into view. John called it 'Sweet Pea'. We would stare into the depths of the pond, waiting for its horrible eyes and slimy body to slide out of the gloom. Its skin was exceptionally smooth. Its staring eyes and sleek buttocks gave it a menacingly sleek appearance. Occasionally it would surface when the pond was teeming with frog spawn and it would get itself entangled in the jelly-like fronds that hung in clumps on the pond's surface. Then we had a chance to see it in all its horror. We crept behind the dome to watch it battle its way out of its entanglement. One hot summer's day John dared me to jump into the pond. It was so hot that I did it that once - but the thought of the toad brushing against my leg still gives me the shivers just thinking about it.

***

The grounds at the superintendent's house included an old tennis court, a disused garage, a corrugated iron shed, a kitchen garden, hundreds of rose bushes, two fish ponds and an orchard. There were oranges, lemons, grapefruit, limes and naartjies in the orchard next to the kitchen garden. We picked strawberries to eat and tomatoes to throw at each other in the summer months. My mother dished up cabbages, lettuces, green beans and potatoes when it was at its most productive. The kitchen garden also provided John and I with an abundant supply of hardened clumps of compost which we used as ammunition in our mud ball fights.

The front lawn went down two tiers of paved steps. The bottom lawn curved along a sweeping flower bed. This was shielded from the bush-land to 23rd Avenue by a plumbago hedge that produced pale blue flowers in the summer. An iron gate in the middle led into an orchard that was tucked away on the edge of the bush. There we could take our pick from guavas, mangos, plums, avocadoes, figs, pomegranates and lychees amongst others. Monique was allergic to mangos so John and I used them to extort prized possessions from her; in my case lipstick, pornographic books and bubble-gum.

11

The servants were scared of things like snakes, spiders, wasps and scorpions. Their beds were raised off the floor with bricks to ward off a particular kind of terror. The Ndebele believe in an evil spirit - the untikolotshe (ontikolotshe in the plural). It is thought to be a hairy creature with gouged out eyes and believed to be no bigger than a small monkey. Our servants said it could bite off their toes while they were asleep. The Ndebele say that its malevolent spirit can cause widespread harm.

***

John used find chameleons in the plumbago hedge. The Africans were terrified of them and rushed off, shouting loudly, to find a broom stick to club them to death. An Ndebele folktale offers an explanation. The tale describes how the Creator God gave the chameleon a message about eternal life and instructed it to give the message to First Man. At the same time, the Creator gave a message about mortality to the lizard. Because chameleons are so slow and hesitant in the way they move, the lizard delivered its message to mankind first. By the time the chameleon arrived, the spring of eternal life had dried up. Even though First Man went on hands and knees and tried to suck its last remaining drops from the earth, there was nothing left. So, to this day in Africa, chameleons are killed because of man's wrath. In order to protect the unfortunate creatures, the Creator endowed chameleons with a magical skin that can change colour; this allows them to disappear into the background. The guards who supervised the squad of inmates working in the garden on weekdays were petrified if an inmate found a chameleon. He would be ordered to kill it by using the sharp end of a heavy iron spade to chop off its head. The blood rushed up into my ears when I caught sight of a chameleon and I ran off in the opposite direction.

Newton and Martin worked as 'guard boys' at Ingutsheni. Every week, Monday to Friday, they brought a group of about five or six African men over from the hospital to work in our garden. The inmates tramped a path with their bare feet as they walked through the mealie field behind our house. They trooped along with one

49

guard at the front and the other at the back. The inmates worked for a few hours in the morning until a gong signalled that it was time for them to file back to the hospital for lunch. They returned for an afternoon shift and then the guards marched them back at five o'clock to be locked up overnight.

John and I used to loiter around the servants' quarters behind the garage where the guards and our servants rolled their cigarettes and sipped their tea out of tin mugs. The inmates sat in a silent group under a tree next to the old tennis court until Martin or Newton sounded the gong and sent them back to do their chores. The guards talked and laughed as they squatted with our servants around the fire, where they shared out bits of newspaper and tobacco to make into cigarettes. Newton's grey moustache with yellowed ends trailed up and down his cigarette as he licked it shut. On cold winter days John and I stood close to the fire and dipped our marie biscuits into their tea. The Africans lit their cigarettes in the coals under a black grate and stood about in the winter sunshine, puffing on them and telling stories with words that clicked and spluttered with laughter.

The inmates swept leaves off the driveway and grass clippings off the lawns with their straw brooms. Monique said their brooms made them look like witches. She said there were witch doctors in Africa. Our granny told us stories about witches who liked to cook children and eat them for dinner. John and I looked at the size of the inmates and decided they were too big to fly around on their brooms. My father said that witchdoctors were a 'bladdy nuisance'. He said they were responsible for making Africans go 'penga' with all their talk of curses and evil doing. He laughed about them throwing bones and said they were a bunch of superstitious black savages. He said the af's had a long way to go before they got anywhere near being as civilised as us. He said that what with bladdy witchdoctors and bladdy prostitutes he was having a hard time coping with the number of mad kaffirs who were being admitted to Ingutsheni.

John and I used to horse around with the inmates and got them to give us piggy backs around the garden. The inmates wore khaki shorts with pale blue shirts and their shaved heads twinkled with beads of sweat as they went about their tasks. Sweat ran in little streams down their cheeks as the sun climbed higher in the sky while the guards stood watching them underneath their wide brimmed hats. In the winter the inmates' legs were covered in goose-bumps because their old brown jumpers were full of holes and they didn't wear knee high khaki socks like the guards. They moved languidly around the garden with an occasional shout or a sudden dance that broke the quietness around them.

Fridays were laundry days and the inmates arrived with clean bundles of laundry on top of their heads. The guards blew their whistles and the caravan of men stopped at the back of the house where they were ordered to put their bundles down outside the kitchen door. The bundles lay where they dropped them, waiting for our servants to unpack them. Our servants stripped our beds and used our dirty sheets to make fresh bundles full of clothes, table cloths and anything else that needed to be washed. They put freshly ironed sheets on our beds and sweet smelling linen around the house; they hung starched towels in the bathroom, and put my father's pressed shirts and our ironed clothes in the cupboards. At the end of the day the bundles were hefted up and the inmates marched solemnly back to the hospital with our dirty laundry on their heads.

Maurice Johnson was in charge of the hospital kitchens and lived at Ingutsheni. I found his son Donald on Facebook. Donald was keen to share his memories with me and sent me a detailed map of the hospital grounds.

Donald wrote:

> *"The white male ward was located behind and was part of the main head office where our Dad's worked. The ward and small recreation area was indeed security fenced. The Native and Asiatics/Coloured wards were bunched together separated by a gravel road. I saw on many occasions native females carrying laundry bundles. There was one female patient who seemed to have no restrictions as she was considered low risk and heavily medicated on Stemetil, rather pleasant to talk to, coherent and polite. Her name was Daisy. There were two white patients of similar classification to Daisy. Tony Bryce, always wore a khaki bush hat also very pleasant to talk to. Then there was Charlie, a Downs Syndrome about twenty years old who used to entertain us with a "guitar" made out of an old "Olivine" tin with a plank attached to it and fishing lines. He used to "play" and sing - a very happy soul as most of them are. We'd*

give him fruit and jam sandwiches which he loved. We all had a real soft spot for him.

Yes I did watch quite a few soccer games and on a number of occasions they'd let me play during practice the day before! As you can see from the sketch there was what appeared to be an old fort which was not visible surrounded by dense scrub. It was a circular structure contained by bricks perfectly laid. They were not normal house bricks but very like the ones at Khami and Zimbabwe ruins. My Dad didn't seem interested when I told him so I wonder if it is still there?

The Bulawayo crematorium was a street or two away from Baines School, can't remember the street names. I don't remember if it was for whites only or there was another one at Mpilo." [Mpilo Hospital, as opposed to the Bulawayo General Hospital, was for non-white patients only. The word "Mpilo" means "life":]"

I had asked Donald if he knew what happened to the inmates when they died. I remember pedalling my bike past the glass doors of the mortuary as I went on my way up the jacaranda avenue to play at an old quarry in the bush. It was on the corner, attached to the high security block. I knew it was a mortuary because there was a hearse parked there most days.

I used to hear people cheering on Sundays at the soccer pitch. When we asked if we could go and watch my father said, "Why would anyone want to go and watch a bunch of kaffirs playing football?"

I used to see a spindly little white woman who took a constitutional walk every afternoon to the hospital entrance. John called her 'little Miss Nit Wit'. She was stick thin and my father said she was 'a bladdy alkie'.

12

The inmates cleaned the cars, polished the veranda and the front steps, weeded my mother's flower beds, planted vegetables, picked fruit and things from the kitchen garden for us to eat, dredged the ponds, killed snakes, destroyed ant hills, mowed the lawns, sprayed pesticides, repaired our bicycles and burned rubbish. My mother's garden task was to spray the roses with sulphur powder when new leaves sprouted in order to keep the green fly at bay. My mother found pleasure in growing roses, and there were nearly two hundred bushes at the superintendent's house. Rectangular beds of pink, cream and white roses surrounded the small fish pond next to Monique's bedroom. Long beds for red and orange roses were dug on either side of the steps which went down to the lower lawn. Names like Largo, Peace, Super Star and Angel Bells bring back instant pictures of the roses that my mother grew and exhibited in the Bulawayo Horticultural Show. She often used to win the rosette for The Best Bowl in the Show.

She and I would wander about the garden as the sun went down and the heat of the afternoon began to lift. I remember how lovely it was to walk with her, enjoying the tranquillity of a dusty carnelian sky at the end of the day. She would snip off a bud and encourage me to smell it before laying it in her basket. I remember the sound of her secateurs and how her enjoyment fed into mine. I lolled on the grass while the sky slowly filled up with the sounds of her graceful snipping and clipping - interspersed with her inhalations and exclamations. In the autumn she pruned them and painted over each stem with her pearly nail varnish to keep out the borer beetles that tunnelled inside the stems where they laid their eggs. I heard the pain in her voice when she found that a beetle had found its way through the varnish. I remember her fury as she hacked the dead branches off, cursing under her breath and leaving the blackened branches on the ground for the inmates to pick up. I watched them scoop up the thorny debri and wheel it off to the rubbish heap near the tennis court to be burned.

During the blistering summers the inmates' main task was to keep the flowerbeds watered. They lined up at the tap and waited while each man dunked his watering-can into a big metal drum. The muscles in their arms bulged and the water left wet trails in the red dust as they slopped off to do their watering. They fitted sprinklers to the ends of their cans and were also made to water the old tennis court with weed killer. Then, two men pulled a heavy metal roller behind the one who was doing the watering. The sweat poured off them and made dark rivers run down their necks and down the backs of their legs. The yellow surface of the court was the same colour as the big cracks inside the backs of their heels. John laughed and said it was the way that God made muntu's feet. Their bare feet got covered over with dust when they swept the driveway. The dust turned their feet pale in just the same way that my mother's talcum powder turned her pubic hair dusty.

The inmates were our constant companions, so much so that my memories of our garden at the big house always include them. I remember only a few of their names: Marupa, and Ntete, and Gonrogh, and Mapicke. Marupa was an old man with white hair.

Monique wrote:

"As soon as you said 'Marupa' I had an image of his thin bony face and soft silvery hair - and that tight dry black skin - funny how one's memory comes back straight away at the name - you're right - he was a quiet dignified man - shame what a life. Of course lots of what you said brought back so many memories that I hadn't given a single thought to for hundreds of years - it really feels like that was someone else's life completely, it's so far removed from today. It also brought back the sadness I used to feel when those poor things lined up for their cigarettes - what a strange life that was for children to have. Anyway I think we've all survived amazingly well."

John wrote:

"I do remember the guards and patients. The guards were Martin and Newton not Nelson. Marupa used to clean the patio and steps - best floor polisher I've ever seen! He did have white hair – he was a sweet man who used to sing whilst he worked. The only other one I remember well was Gonrogh – we used to call him Gone Wrong – he used to work tirelessly and shouted loudly every now and then.

Martin always used to tell me his bicycle was a motor bike and that Elspeth was his transistor radio! He wasn't as friendly as Newton, he was also sterner with the patients".

Mapicke was young and strong and he was exceptionally silent. So obliging was he that the guards used him for all the strenuous chores that needed to be done. It was Mapicke who dug the square holes with an iron pick axe when my mother pointed out to the guards where she wanted to plant a new rose bush. It was Mapicke who mowed the lawns, helped pull the roller on the tennis court and humped heavy wheelbarrows around the garden. Like all the other inmates, his eyes looked as if they'd been dyed orange in the bits that should have been white. The whites of Ntete's eyes were a blood orange and his bottom lids were as deep red as the pomegranate pips that John and I spat at each other in the orchard. There was a sweet medicinal smell about all of them, mixed in with a strong whiff of body odour. I was acutely aware of this when they gave us piggy backs around the garden; they stank to high heaven.

During a mud ball fight with John, I accidentally hit Ntete in the face. I stood and watched him shaking his shaved head like a dog does when a fly lands somewhere bothersome. He stood stock still for a moment, making little clicking noises, and then a stream of unintelligible words came out of his mouth. I did not see that I had drawn blood because his skin was such a dark black. I realised he was bleeding when he turned his head and the sun glinted in the blood running down the side of his face. When I got up close to him I saw a nasty red dent in his forehead. Ntete did not cry or hold his head; he carried on sweeping with his broom making the little clicking sounds with his tongue. He was a small barrel of a person and the skin on his face was so lumpy that he seemed to have a permanent case of the goose-bumps. I felt a bit sheepish at what I had done but nobody seemed to mind. The guard boys, if they witnessed it, turned a blind eye. John had long since disappeared. The thrill of the chase was over and I knew no one would bother to tell my parents.

***

I remember one of my mother's friends looking me up and down before she got into her car one afternoon. She'd spent the afternoon gossiping and sipping tea with my mother underneath the shelter in the garden. My mother had a habit of making John and I come and say goodbye to visitors. Her friend said: "You've got very nice legs, you know, Cait." Then she turned to my mother and said "I don't know why you let John and Cait play with those crazy kaffirs Elspeth – really!" She held her handkerchief up to her nose and rolled her eyes.

***

One Easter Sunday my mother was furious when she discovered that the inmates had found the Easter eggs she'd hidden around the garden, and had eaten them as they went about their chores. John and I realised that if our mother was the Easter Bunny that she was very likely Father Christmas as well. A week or so before Christmas, we climbed up the back of the garage wall and peered through the rafters into the little storeroom behind. There we saw all our Christmas presents, waiting to be wrapped.

13

One night someone broke into the big house.

John wrote:

> *"Can't recall much about that night. All I remember was being woken by the sound of the window being pushed open. It had been left ajar. I remember seeing the burglar's head and watching him pull himself up onto the window sill. He was very agile. He stood on the sill for a very short time and then jumped into our room. He walked past our beds and into the next room. I then heard Norman shouting and several bangs as the burglar slammed the door into the sitting room and Norman tried to open it whilst the burglar held it shut from the other side. That's about it."*

Monique remembers how the police came the next morning and dusted everywhere for finger prints. She wrote:

> *"I do remember the robbery/break in at the big house. I think the fellow also stole Norman's tin with the dog on top of it but don't know where that was. I didn't think it was a patient because they didn't go outside until a certain time and this happened either in the night or very early morning - around three or four in the morning. I wish I had a clearer memory but know it was a very scary experience."*

I remember, like Monique, that the burglar stole my father's money box. Since he kept it in the top drawer of his desk in the study, my memory is that my father was locked in his study. For weeks after the burglary, as I wandered along my favourite paths in the bush, or pedalled around the hospital grounds, I kept an eye out for my father's money box. I knew that he kept a silver revolver in the same drawer as the money box and was glad that he didn't shoot the burglar. I wondered why the burglar hadn't picked up the revolver when he stole the box, because it was still there the next time I looked in the drawer. Just to be on the safe side, I took all my loose change and put it in one of my mother's old biscuit tins. Then I dug a hole in the bush near the kitchen garden and buried it. I guess it's still there.

Monique added:

> *"What I remember more clearly was Moses being in a fight and Norman going out with his little gun then taking poor Moses off to the police station but I don't think it was his fault - it was a fight caused by some other person who had either wandered in or had come back from drinking with Moses but again it was a scary experience.*

***

One hot afternoon, when the cicadas were making a white noise in the sky, I stole a box of matches out of the kitchen and set fire to a dry tuft of pine needles on a fir tree at the top of the drive. John and I stepped back in horror as the whole branch ignited. The tree turned into a fire ball and we knew we were in serious trouble. The blare of the cicadas rang in our ears as we scampered off to the hospital farm to hide. We stayed there and waited until our stomachs told us it was time to head home for supper. My mother said she had called the fire brigade because the bush had gone up in flames and the fire had spread rapidly all the way to 23rd Avenue. The next morning the house was surrounded by a black wasteland which still emitted wisps of white smoke. The blaze was so fierce that it had also burned down the plumbago hedge. The ground crunched underneath our feet when we went to survey the damage. My father said that he was sure one of the servants had started it by throwing away a cigarette. He said they were stupid and careless, always setting fire to things. He said it was because the black bastards couldn't read and there were plenty of signs around town warning people about throwing cigarettes into the bush. I remember how John and I had looked at each other in relief.

14

My life changed dramatically in 1963 when a new family came to live in the little house next door. To my everlasting joy, their daughter Roseanna was the same age as me and it wasn't very long before we became close friends. Her parents, Roger and Trudy, welcomed me and John into their family with open arms. Roseanna's older brothers, Sean and Dillon, were distant but friendly. Roseanna, with her freckled face, auburn curls and the same pointy nose as her father, opened up a world I'd not encountered before.

John became known as 'John the Baptist' over at the Baxter's house. Roger and Trudy were devout Catholics and they said "God bless" when we came over to visit and when we went home again. Roseanna and her brothers wore their best clothes to Sunday school and they looked as smart as we did when my mother booked for us to eat at The Peking Chinese Restaurant for our birthdays. I remember Roseanna's confirmation and the tiara she wore in her hair. I remember how her black shoes shone in the sunshine. She told me that illegitimate children weren't blessed. They went to limbo first and then to purgatory where they roasted in Hell. She said that the ones at St. Francis Home had been rescued by the nuns so they were lucky not to be in limbo or being roasted by the devil for being wicked. She said sinners were people who did bad things and unless they said they were very sorry to God every time they committed a sin, they were in big trouble when they died. She said sinners hadn't reached a state of grace by doing penalties to say they were sorry, and so they joined all the illegitimate children and bad people in Hell. She had a big silver cross on the wall above her bed and a picture of Jesus with his chest torn open and a crown of thorns on his head that made blood pour down his face. Jesus was hanging on a cross and had a big gash in his side too.

Roger was a sandy-haired man with pale green eyes and a spattering of orange freckles all over his face. Trudy's beehive hairstyle made her seem taller than my mother. She liked fuchsia coloured lipstick that looked very bright next to a chocolate mole above her mouth and her green eyes smiled when she talked. Her nails matched her lipstick and she wore a perfume that smelt of apples.

Trudy had two Siamese cats called Minoo and Lily and I often heard her calling for them in the evenings when it was getting dark. She said there were snakes in the bush and she couldn't rest until the cats were safe and sound inside the house. Trudy taught us to make stained glass pictures out of old sheets of glass. She smoothed a collection of sweet wrappers into shiny squares to stick on the reverse side. Roseanna, John and I spent hours choosing colours from a tin, to stick onto the pictures she drew for us. She also made pewter frames decorated with flowers and birds which she fixed around mirrors and works of art. Our old house became a happy port of call after school and on the weekends. Roseanna and her family lit a creative spark for me that has never diminished.

The Baxters inherited the Wright's metal swimming tank next to the old tennis wall. We were desperate to swim in it on hot summer days so my mother sent me and John for lessons with Mrs Van der Merwe at the Borrow Street swimming pool. Near the pool, in Lobengula Street, was Mrs Coetzee's house, where my mother took me to have my dresses made. Jacoba Coetzee was the seamstress at Ingutsheni. She was an Afrikaner woman whose nose looked like a purple carbuncle. She took my measurements with a filthy old tape measure while she puffed on a cigarette in the side of her mouth. 'Old Coetz' stank of beer and the bruises on her face matched the colour of her nose. Our swimming teacher, Mrs Van der Merwe, was a younger version of Old Coetz because she spoke with an Afrikaans accent. Mrs Van's deeply tanned skin gave her a leathery look. Her cropped hair was speckled with streaks of brown, orange and yellow. Mrs Van instructed us to hold onto a plank of wood, on one end of which was a long piece of rope. Holding the rope in one hand, she would pick me up and shout "hold tight and shut your mouth" into my ear. Then she threw me into the pool like a bag of potatoes and set off at a steady along the side. I sailed along on the end of her rope, swallowing water as I went. Mrs Van yelled at me "to kick for bladdy Africa", then left me to pound my way aimlessly around the pool until she blew her whistle. After several 'lessons' she decided the time had come to snatch the wood out of my hands, and all that I had learned became a test of survival. Over those agonising weeks, I would look up at John as he waited for his turn in his little Speedo swimming costume. He stood with his fingers in his ears as I splashed and cried my way around the pool. His turn soon came to be thrown into the water, clutching on to his piece of wood, and he too learned "to kick for bladdy Africa" in double quick time.

When I remember all the fun we had swimming with Roseanna and her family, Mrs Van der Merwe and her swimming lessons pale into insignificance. We spent hours climbing up on to the side of the tank and throwing ourselves into the water. The joy of swimming turned even our bath times into fun times. One evening John was rolling around on top of me in the bath, when my father rushed in, pulled him off and smacked him very hard on the bottom. Then he hauled me out and hit me too, as hard as he could. He shouted at us and then disappeared. He clearly thought that we were having sex in the bath but was too enraged or embarrassed to ask us what we were doing. He was not to know that we were playing at being whales just as we did in the Baxter's tank.

We learned to keep out of my father's way when we played games around the house. He disapproved of what he called 'showing off'. I was never sure when I had overstepped his definition of what this meant and braced myself for a hiding.

15

My mother wrote:

> *"The Baxters came about 1963 – they were a mixed religion family.*
> *Trudy took the kids to Mass (R.C.) and Roger was a C. of E. person.*
> *Trudy played tennis and was really keen – she pressed me to allow*
> *you to go to classes with Colonel Perkins at Suburbs on Saturday*
> *afternoon. I thought you were too young, but said "Yes" – and hoped*
> *for you to decide. To my delight you enjoyed playing and Colonel*
> *and Mrs Perkins thought you had a natural talent – and so we were*
> *happy. Norman willingly paid for coaching for Lesley and you and*
> *subsequently John. Monique was not at all interested in sport."*

Trudy made me and Roseanna a pair of matching tennis dresses. I
remember her taking us into town to choose the fabric. My dress was
sleeveless, with a round-necked bodice, a low waist and a gathered
skirt. Trudy made a little pocket above the skirt, just big enough to
hold a tennis ball. She edged the waist and the pocket with a thin
ribbon that had blue, red and green flowers embroidered on it. I loved
the way my dress swung around my hips as well as the blue and
white frilly knickers she made to go underneath. My mother bought
me a Maxply tennis racquet that smelled like her clear nail polish. It
had a red leather handle. She said the strings were yellow because
they were made of cat gut. It smelt intoxicatingly meaty.

Colonel Ramsey Perkins was a retired British army officer. He was
a tall man with twinkling blue eyes and a bushy moustache. His arms
and legs were tanned a deep nut brown against his white shorts. He
wore white takkies, white socks with blue stripes at the top and a
white shirt. Even when the sun made the sand on the tennis court
shimmer and the cicadas sang like alarm bells, the Colonel wore his
creamy woollen pullover with its cable patterns and the badge on it
that said 'Fred Perry'. He wore a battered old khaki hat and his sun
glasses were black underneath it. He stood next to one of the posts at
the net and held himself erect. Ramsey Perkins had played county
tennis before the war and he said we all had the potential to play in
the Wimbledon Tennis Championships if we obeyed his instructions.
He wore an enormous gold ring on his little finger. He and my

mother got on like a house on fire and she called him 'dear Ramsey' when she spoke of him.

Roseanna and I skidded around on the sandy court while the Colonel told us how to hold our racquets and when to swing at the ball. I remember him being extremely patient. He would often walk over to hold an arm and demonstrate the way to swing, adjust a grip or position a foot. We watched in awe as he hit a ball over the net with effortless accuracy and we gazed in wonder at the power of his serves. He could smash balls with precision and then amble up to the net like a graceful giraffe. He volleyed back the balls we hit at him with the nonchalance of the old hand that he was.

The Colonel used an electric machine which made a rattling noise like a machine gun. It had a firing arm which hit balls over the net at varying speeds. The machine had a wire basket at the top, and as each ball was fired, another dropped down into position. The arm was fitted to a big metal spring which had to be adjusted manually. The Colonel employed two young Africans named Willard and Maxim to operate the machine and they each had bulging muscles on their bare arms. They man-handled the machine on its iron wheels, pushing it at angles as instructed by the Colonel. Maxim was a bit younger than Willard and I remember he fired the machine with more precision and power than Willard did. The Colonel taught them to play tennis, and as the years went by Willard regularly took part in playing games against us. Maxim's serves made the ball zing past our ears to embed itself in the fence behind us. Willard was much kinder when he played with us and he listened to the Colonel's rules about being a good sport and a gentleman. Willard wore the same kind of khaki hat that the Colonel wore and he also had a big gold ring on his little finger. Willard and Maxim took turns at collecting the balls around the court and they helped each other load up the machine for the next round of shots.

The Colonel's wife Annabel sat next to the net in a deck chair. She was a tiny woman with grey wispy hair hidden under the brim of her sun hat. My mother said that Annabel was very quiet because she had lost both her children in the war. She clicked her tongue when she told us and said that Annabel sipped gin out of her thermos flask because you didn't ever get over a thing like that. Mrs Perkins used to let me and Roseanna stroke the mouse brooch she wore on the front of her hat. She said it was made of mink. She wore bright red lipstick and some of it was smudged on her front teeth. When my mother told me about the gin, I realised that it was Annabel's breath that stank and not her mousey brooch.

At the end of our lessons, while we waited for our mothers to collect us, the Colonel gave us orange juice in paper cups. He poured himself a cup of tea out of his thermos. He ate his sandwiches and gave us talks about tactics. While he munched on his sandwiches, the Colonel also conducted a presentation ceremony. Every week it was possible for one of us to win a gold badge. The winner was the person who had the highest score of balls over the net and into court. Ten badges added up to a gold tie pin. Ten gold tie pins earned a match, the best of three games, against the Colonel himself the following week. He seldom lost a point, but when he did, he always said the same thing: "Keep that up and I'll be watching you hold the Wimbledon Singles Trophy above your head one day." Willard and Maxim re-painted the lines on the court while the Colonel held the presentation ceremony. They mixed the whitewash in a tin can with a stick and then poured it into a machine on wheels. Willard stood at one end of a baseline and Maxim pulled some string into a straight line. Once the string was hammered in place, the little machine was pushed along on its wheels. It smelled the same as the white wash our servants used on my takkies to keep them looking new.

I spent hours practising my strokes against the back of the servants' quarters. I whacked tennis balls from the top lawn to the bottom lawn and hit them so hard and so high that they sailed over the house and into the fruit orchard behind the kitchen. I bounced a ball up and down on the strings until I lost count. I practised flicking my racquet out of my hand and catching it on the handle like I'd seen the cowboys in Bonanza doing with their guns. After a while, the Colonel told my mother that I was showing great promise and suggested that I start having private lessons with him. So I went along for an hour on a Saturday morning when there was not another soul at the Suburbs Tennis Club and I had the Colonel and his machine all to myself.

I won the Matabeleland Under Twelve Girls Singles in 1966. The Colonel pronounced me "Queen Victoria of the tennis court". I was chosen to play for Matabeleland when I was thirteen. The Bulawayo Chronicle ran a story with the heading: "Little Caitie saves Face for Matabeleland". I remember staring at my name and my photograph on the page with a mixture of disbelief and pleasure. My father said I must be careful not to let it go to my head. John started having lessons with the Colonel too and soon we were hitting tennis balls at each other as well as throwing mud balls and tomatoes.

Roseanna's enthusiasm for tennis was not as great as mine so we went off on our bikes to play amongst the tomato plants at the hospital farm. When John was with us, we threw rotten ones at each other and played hide and seek in the disused barns.

***

Roseanna and I used to cycle over to an old quarry near the St. Francis Home. We left our bikes at the top and slid our way down its sandy sides on our bottoms. We never dared swim in the stagnant water because my father said we'd get sleeping sickness from bilharzia and never wake up. One day, when we were playing down at the water's edge, I got a tremendous fright. A movement in the grasses peeping over the edge of the quarry caught my eye and I saw a group of inmates ducking and diving their way through the bush. One of them caught sight of us and signalled me to be quiet. Then their silhouettes peered down at us and I grabbed Roseanna by the arm. We scuttled out of sight and hid ourselves away. We stayed there for ages before we found the courage to make a run for it and scamper back up to the top. We grabbed our bikes and pedalled home as fast as we could. In our panic we were not sure who or what we had seen. I told Roseanna they must have been Red Indians and Roseanna said "No" she was pretty sure they were leprechauns. We agreed not to tell our parents and it took us a while before we felt brave enough to play at the quarry once more.

After Roseanna and her family moved away, I never went to the quarry again.

16

John remembers that he and I went swimming at the Baxter's house the day before Roger died.

He wrote:

> *"I remember swimming with you in the Baxter's pool on the Saturday. Roger Baxter was with us in the pool. On Sunday afternoon, Norman took me to the boating pond in the Bulawayo park to make me feel better. That is all I remember."*

I remember it was sweltering hot that Saturday. I was happy to stay and swim on my own after Roger got out of the pool and John scampered back home. I jumped off the side of the tank onto Roseanna's lilo. I must have landed next to the seal because it let out a hiss and sank into the choppy water. I was afraid that I'd broken it and was sure I'd get into trouble. So I stayed bobbing up and down, too afraid to take the useless lilo to Roger and explain what had happened. It is sad thinking back to that day and the fact that when I finally climbed out of the pool, I was too embarrassed to go and say thank you to him. I never saw Roger or any of his family again.

I wrote and asked my mother to tell me what she remembered about Roger's death. She wrote:

> *"The Baxters were a strange crowd – the children were very disturbed by the religious teaching. I remember Roseanna frightening you with stories of purgatory and being "in limbo" if you died without being in a "state of grace".*
>
> *As for Roger's death. You and John went swimming on Sat p.m. and I had invited Roger for lunch on the following day. Trudy and the kids were in Cape Town with her mother and he was alone over Christmas and New Year. On Sunday a.m. I told our servants Roger would be here for lunch and what to make etc., and went to have a bath. Their servant came up to say she could not find Roger and I told her to look for the car because he was probably in one of the wards. I said I would come over so I got out of the bath, dressed and walked over. As I came near to the Little House I smelt ether. I remember being anxious and walked into the house thro' the back door. I called and walked to the main bedroom. The bed had been*

slept in and the light was on – unusual because it was light. Then I knocked on the bathroom door – it was locked. I went outside to try to see thro' the window. By now I was really worried – so I tried to find Norman on the ward, and by great luck I found him talking to Dennis Peterson (a senior doctor in Rhodesia – President of the Medical Council). I told Norman the situation and asked them both to come over. I phoned Lesley and asked her to restrain you and John from coming over – because I didn't want you two to come and find the Police, etc. Anyway eventually the Police broke the window and Roger was dead in the bath, with a plastic bag over his head. Dr Montgomery explained that Roger had been with them for dinner on Saturday night and they had discussed a theory that certain psychoses were eased by causing brief unconsciousness with the use of ether, in patients. So no-one could decide if Roger's death was accidental or a suicide.

I remember coming back to our house and dear Lesley sat me down – made me tea – made me toast – and she comforted me – because I was very upset by this event, and dreaded Trudy's return and reactions. However, all was well – Trudy took herself back to Cape Town, the children stayed with their grandmother.

Eventually, she married Rupert and so far as I know they now all live in South Africa. The little house was occupied by the Chief Nursing Officer after that. We did not tell you or John about suicide, etc but that Roger had had a heart attack – you both shed a few tears. That's all I can tell you."

Roger died on Sunday 3rd January 1965. I still have two beloved books which Roseanna gave me. The first one is called *A Friend is Someone Who Likes You* by Joan Walsh Anglund. The other one is also by Joan Walsh Anglund - *A Pocketful of Proverbs*. It is a miniature book with a line drawing on every page. It slips inside a hard cover pocket with a patchwork design on it. On the back, in red letters, I have written: "*Cait Fine. Given to me by Roseanna 20.7.66.*" Trudy either posted *The Pocketful of Proverbs* to me or, what is more likely, she brought it with her when she came to Bulawayo for the inquest into Roger's death. When I look at Joan Anglund's miniature books, I can see that it was not so much the words that appealed to me. It is the lovely pen and ink illustrations of children. Losing the Baxters, and especially my friend Roseanna, was a terrible blow.

The date on the back of the book is significant because it's the day after my eleventh birthday. I remember my mother had given it to me earlier, when I was very ill. My father said that I had the measles and I remember my mother laughing and saying that it was a fateful date because it was 6.6.66. It was the only time I got to sleep through the night in my parents' bed. I remember having hallucinations and seeing little green men running all over the eiderdown. My mother sat next to me with a bowl of iced water and sponged my forehead with icy bits of cotton wool. She gave me Roseanna's present to read while I lay in bed.

I remember writing the inscription on the back of the book once I'd recovered. It was the second anniversary of having a birthday without Roseanna there to share it with me.

17

My father's job as a psychiatrist at Ingutsheni meant that he sat on the Mental Health Board of Rhodesia. He was involved in the judiciary and had connections with the British South Africa Police. When John and I went to play tennis in Salisbury for the first time, we stayed with the sister of the Commissioner of the British South Africa Police. Her daughter was the same age as John. I remember being wary of their police dog, a German Shepherd named Shaka. I stayed with a Magistrate, whose son also played tennis for Mashonaland. His father held mine in high esteem and I still have a book of essays he gave me, written by some of the eminent thinkers of the early twentieth century.

***

On 11th November 1965, the Prime Minister of Rhodesia, Ian Douglas Smith declared Unilateral Independence (UDI) from Great Britain. It is possible to listen again to Smith speaking on the Rhodesian Broadcasting Corporation website. Smith had been a fighter pilot with the Royal Air Force during World War Two. He suffered terrible injuries to his face and body as a result of being shot down over enemy territory. Smith had a slurpy way of speaking: *"We, the Europeans, we are all powerful. We have the reins in our hands and we can pretty much do what we like."*

I remember my mother telling me about UDI as we drove home one day from school. She said that UDI meant no more imported chocolate or cigarettes. The Rhodesians invented a brand of chocolates called Charons and cigarettes in a pale blue box called Kingsgate. Both brought mutterings from my parents. We had no choice but to succumb to the sanctions imposed on Rhodesia. My father shook his head about the growing 'communist threat' and he said that 'the terrorists who hid in the Tribal Trust Lands were causing a bladdy lot of carnage'. He shook his head and said 'good old Smithy would sort out the blacks'. There were programmes on the radio for 'our boys in the bush' defending the country out in the sweltering bush where not only 'gooks' lurked but wild animals too. Daniel Carney wrote a book called 'The Whispering Death'. It told the story about an albino terrorist leader who was eventually tracked down and killed by a captain in the Selous Scouts. There was a bloody fight to the death in a dry river bed.

I used to ride my bike over to the Bradfield shops where I spent hours flipping through magazine-type stories with black and white photographs of 'our boys', armed with AK 47's. Their mission was to seek out and kill those responsible for the atrocities which were photographed in graphic detail on the pages that I stood and gawped at. There were pictures of dead Europeans – men, women and children with their throats cut and their bodies dismembered, lying in big black pools of dried blood. There were photos of bullet riddled cars with dead Europeans slumped half in and half out of open doors, with blood dripping down their lifeless faces.

***

After UDI nobody stood to attention any more in the cinema when the British National Anthem was played. I remember how my mother took me and my sisters to see The Sound of Music when I was about ten years old and I obediently rose out of my seat as God Save the Queen began to play. Clearly the powers that be had forgotten to edit the films that were smuggled in from England after Ian Smith's momentous declaration and I was roughly tugged back down by someone seated behind me. Monique glared at me and my mother shifted uncomfortably in her seat.

***

Towards the end of 1965, a new hall was built at Ingutsheni. I wore my pale blue dress with silver smocking across the top to go to the opening concert with my parents. I remember sitting cross legged on the floor with all the other children who lived at Ingutsheni. Mr Radcliffe came over with a microphone and knelt down beside me. He asked me to sing Eidelweiss with him. I knew that it came from The Sound of Music but I didn't know any of the words. I wished the floor would swallow me up because Mr Radcliffe stayed and sang the whole thing with me sitting on his knee. Years later I learned that George Radcliffe was accused of sexually molesting a young boy on one of the wards but no charges were pressed by the superintendent.

***

In 1966 my mother got a pale green Citroen whose silver bumpers glittered in the sunshine. It looked like a frog. It had RBC13 printed in big white letters on its number plate. John said it stood for the 'Rhodesian Broadcasting Corporation'. Its power steering made my mother's handling of the car seem totally effortless. It had hydraulic brakes that sighed when she stepped on them and the car would glide obediently to a halt. Its most remarkable feature was that it rose up and floated on a bed of air when a little lever on the floor next to the driver's seat was pressed down. John and I delighted when she made the car rise up like a magic carpet. It sailed gracefully over the enormous humps across Bulawayo's wide streets like a hover craft. The humps were created so that rain water flowed away into ditches and storm drains after the cloud-bursts that flooded the city centre. After John and I learned to drive, we used to aquaplane through the miniature lakes that grew on either side of the humps in my father's little white Mini.

I remember when John was having driving lessons that his driving instructor warned him to "watch out for the jungle bunnies" referring to the Africans who were always about in the industrial areas where he took John to practise his three-point turns and his reversing.

18

The senior male nurse and his family who replaced the Baxters were known by my parents as 'little Willy wooden head and the gang'. When my mother's friend Denise came to stay from England and hummed little tunes to herself as she meandered around our house, my father christened her 'dear old dumb-dumb'. My father hummed little tunes in his Mini when he took me to school. He would give me a wink accompanied by a mischievous smile. "Ah, good old dumb-dumb" he would murmur as we drove along. We all caught the habit from him. 'Little miss bottom' regularly beat me at tennis, 'thunderbolt' was a man with a powerful service action, 'lobster' was one of John's tennis friends who went red and lobbed balls into the sky to slow the game down, 'rudder' was a Jewish boy with a big nose, 'pacer' was a girl who never varied her game, 'pink panther' was a skinny boy with a wide smile, 'warthog' grunted when he delivered a serve and 'the convict' was John's friend who wore a striped jumper. My tennis friends Sally and Debbie were known as 'Silly and 'Dilly'.

**

After I lost Roseanna, I struggled to make a new friend. Few parents were brave enough to let their children come over and play with me at the lunatic asylum. Eventually my mother engineered a friendship for me at school. Amelia's father was a furniture restorer. My mother knew Derek Hobson via her friend Winifred. It turned out that Derek's daughter was in my class, and Amelia's granny was our teacher. I guess they took pity on me when my mother told them that I had lost my friend next door. The Hobson's lived in a large bungalow in Suburbs and I was invited over for barbeques and games. I loved playing charades at Amelia's house because the grown-ups took such an interest in us children. She had a big extended family. I was amazed that the adults joined in our games when we swam around in the swimming pool together. Everyone laughed and gave each other hugs, including her father and her uncles. They slapped each other on the back while they stood around the fire, smoking and drinking their beers.

One weekend I was invited to go camping with Amelia and another friend from school. Off we went to West Nicholson in a jeep, with a trailer bumping along behind us. We drove off the tarred strips that served as a road and careered through the bush until we found a good spot to put up the tents. The three of us slept in a row inside a big canvas tent next to a clump of thorn trees. I met a baby at breakfast the next morning, but I shied away when its mother offered for me to hold it. It was wearing a pale blue dressing gown and had just thrown up all down its front.

The first night was exciting because it rained, and we woke up smelling the damp earth. We lay and listened to birds and animals calling to one another in the bush. By the second night I wasn't very happy to be there at all. Amelia's father and the other men in the party had unpacked their hunting rifles and had gone out in the jeep to shoot game. They came back in time for lunch with a dead kudu tied to the top of the jeep. Later on I was horrified to see its skinned, headless carcass hanging on a branch near our tent. There was a gaping hole down its middle and clouds of flies hung around black innards that lay on a tarp. I overheard Amelia's father laughing that they had killed two birds with one stone and was distraught to find out that the kudu had been pregnant. They had dumped the baby on the ground near its mother's carcass. I went off into the bush with my camera and spent a long while taking photographs on my own. When I got back to the camp, a fire had been lit and the men were well on their way to getting drunk.

There was more shooting the following morning and the kudu was joined by a string of dead guinea fowl and another small antelope with its head cut off. Lunch involved further drinking so the drive back to Amelia's house was pretty hair-raising. When my mother picked me up on Sunday evening, I clung to my seat belt and begged her not to drive like Amelia's father.

19

My mother wrote:

> *"Why did you run away and hide when we lived at Ingutsheni? Was it because you were too scared to face an angry parent? Or was it to punish presumably me – for accusing you? I've never understood the motive for your running off – over several years. You asked me, in a letter, about why I was frightened when you "ran away". Well, it was partly because of the environment – seven hundred acres of bush, and some of the inhabitants were known to be crazy in one way or another. Also there were hazards in the animal and reptile species at Ingutsheni – as well as the quarry, sometimes filled to some level with water. All these hazards were fact – but also I didn't understand what made you "take off" – if you were angry, frightened, what went on inside your head? Lots of children "run off" but most announce their intention. I used to do it as a child myself – which gave my mother time to pack a tiny attaché case, take me by the hand and push me and the case out of the front door, say "good-bye" and shut the door firmly on me. This was such a shock to me that I set off defiantly, but by the time I reached the gate to the lane we lived on, I was too attached to my home to go further. But you didn't do that – you just vanished."*

I never went very far in the beginning. The big house was set apart from the other houses at Ingutsheni and so it was easy for me to disappear into the bush just beyond the periphery of the garden. I found refuge in places where I could sit, hidden away under the canopy of a tree. I stayed there for ages hoping that my mother would search for me. I was soon engrossed in all the comings and goings of the world around me. I could feast my eyes on beautiful sunbirds, swallowtail butterflies, iridescent wasps and speckled guinea fowl. Eventually I made my way back home when I got hungry. When I was older I would pedal my bike over to the hospital farm or ride over to the Bradfield shops. I often disappeared by climbing trees. I would sit up high, not thinking of anything in particular, while the motion of the branch and the comings and goings around me lulled me into a world of my own away from my family.

***

Lesley left home on 12th September 1966 and she has never been back to Africa. John remembers the day that Lesley left more clearly than I do. He says we went out for a farewell meal at the Bulawayo Southern Sun where he and I shared a smoked salmon starter. He remembers that he and Lesley sipped champagne with Monique and my parents. The next morning we drove to the station in two cars so that we could all say goodbye. John says that he, my father and Lesley walked to the luggage car where they stowed away the grey suitcases with leather patches on the corners that my mother had bought at Haddon and Sly.

I have a faint memory of seeing my nineteen-year-old sister looking out at me from the carriage window as we waited for the guard to blow the whistle. As the train slowly pulled away I was not to know what her departure meant or how long it would be before I saw her again. She left that spring morning on a train that took her to Cape Town, where she boarded the Edinburgh Castle and sailed to Southampton. She journeyed on by train to take up her place at Durham University to study languages.

In 1970, Lesley caused some shock waves at home. She gave away all the money my mother had siphoned into a savings account for her. She donated over £3,000 to the Peruvian earthquake disaster fund. I remember telling my friends at school what a great humanitarian gesture my sister had made. Lesley turned into a distant heroine because what she did scandalised my parents to the extent that it did. When I turned thirteen, she sent me The Missa Luba, a recording of a Congolese choir singing in a church. Ever since I've loved the sound of African drumming and the beauty of African voices singing a cappella.

When I went on holiday to the UK in 1978, the bespectacled dark-haired woman who came to meet me at York station one hot summer's day was a stranger. I had knitted Lesley a winter scarf in anticipation of meeting her again but it didn't warm the thirteen years that stretched between us like a tightrope. As she walked me and my ridiculously heavy suitcase to her flat, I sweated in my brown tweed trouser suit and struggled to know what to say. She was so English in the way she spoke. Lesley was so utterly different from

Monique with whom I had shared so much more of my life that I instantly felt at sea with her. It didn't help that her flatmates were French speakers. I felt like a fish out of water.

After Lesley left home, Monique was given my parents' old bedroom, and they took over Lesley's double room with its door onto the side garden and its inner storage space. I was given Monique's old bedroom with its pale blue wooden shutters, delicate green walls and lavender bedspread. After the burglary I felt safer at night with the shutters shut tight and the door locked.

I've often wished I'd had the freedom that Lesley had by being able to pick up her British nationality where she left off, and to get on with life away from Ingutsheni and our parents. My experience has been very different.

***

One hot afternoon a little white cat fell out of the bougainvillea near the front door and landed at my feet. I coaxed her into my room and, after lots of persuasion and regular meals, she became my faithful companion. I named her Kitty and spent hours grooming and petting her in my new bedroom. I could not get to sleep until I had locked Kitty in with me. If I couldn't feel her solid little weight on my feet at the end of my bed, a fearful panic gripped at my heart. Then, I ran about outside, calling her name with desolate longing. Once, when it was already dark, I went out on to the top lawn, my voice growing hollower and hollower with need. I stood on something which felt like the garden hose. When it wriggled under my bare foot, I knew it was a snake. Then I flew back to the house and sat shivering on my bed. I dreamed a black mamba had swallowed my purring friend. And, in the morning, when her small white form once more greeted my eye, my heart went back into its normal rhythm. With joy and relief, I held her close and stroked her soft fur. When I heard the motor start up inside her throat I felt reassured that she was back to stay. Her presence guaranteed that the sun would shine and I knew that the next day, and the day after that, would be full of ordinary pleasures.

Kitty was bright white in the blazing sunshine. I could feel her ribs when I clutched her. She was always out hunting for things in the long grass beyond the plumbago hedge. I knew when she'd brought in one of her kills because Monique would let out a scream. Then there would be an almighty fuss until one of the servants came and grabbed the dead thing away from the cat and flung it outside. Or else my mother would come running and chase Kitty outside with her prey dangling out of her mouth. Once far enough away, Kitty would crouch in the undergrowth, growling while she crunched up her meal. My father hated my cat. Whenever he found her asleep in the lounge or lying on the warm veranda in the evenings he hissed at her so that she ran off. Underneath Kitty's snowy fur, she was covered in ticks. My mother would instruct me to pull the ticks off while she lit up a cigarette. I would drop each miniature blue sack with its waving legs into her ashtray. My mother would incinerate each one with a pop. To this day, alongside the smell of cigarette smoke comes the pungent memory of burnt cat fur – and a curious satisfaction of a job well done.

A few years Kitty's arrival, John found a grey cat in the bush beyond the hedge. His cat was just as wild as Kitty had been, and he called him Crazy Greyzie. Crazy Greyzie was savage in ways that always took us by surprise. I could tell when Kitty was going to bite me because her pupils suddenly went a hundred times bigger than normal. With John's cat there was no such warning and our hands were riddled with puncture marks and scratches. My mother's nursing skills came to the fore, and she dressed our wounds with bright red mercurochrome ointment.

When we got mouth ulcers, she opened up her medicine box and dabbed at them with gentian violet. After I'd been swimming and my ears got blocked, she reached for her silver syringe. I sat on the kitchen stool, holding a kidney dish against my head. My mother filled the syringe with warm water and pushed my head over to one side. I sat as still as a statue and marvelled at my mother's steady hand as the warm surge of water jetted inside my ear. After several rounds she instructed me to tilt my head the opposite way and jump the remaining water out of my ear like a kangaroo. My sudden ability to hear once more was matched by the joy of examining all the wax that had shot out of my ear, floating in its little silver pond.

***

John and I often pedalled over to the farm - past the female ward, along the crunchy cinder track which went behind the wards and laundry, until we came to the fields where the barns and the old cattle sheds stood empty. Pungent animal smells, clods of manure and bits of hay swirled around in the hot air. Dried cow pats and clouds of flies drifted with fine drops of water from the sprinklers that spat in the distance. We entered a peaceful other world. Sometimes we saw inmates toiling in the fields where rows of crops - mealies, tomatoes, runner beans, spinach and potatoes - grew in abundance. Guards stood around with their knobkerries dangling off their belts and their polished boots glistening in the sun. They wore their khaki hats with leather straps under their chins to keep the sun off their heads. The farm tractor and its trailer waited to ferry the men and the produce they picked back to the hospital. Sometimes we found the farm deserted. Then we would chase each other across the fields. We would throw mud balls, and tomatoes, and whatever else was close to hand at each other. I remember the sweet aroma that leaked out of the thick outer coverings around ripe mealies. The yellow corn inside its hairy inner layer lay incubating in the sun like an exotic treasure. The stringy tangle of hairs brought with it the sensual pleasure of finding something sweet-smelling and forbidden.

20

I was horrified when my tennis friend Lucy Miller was killed in a car crash. I took myself off into the bush where I drew an enormous star in the sand. I sang the Beatles' song Lucy in the Sky with Diamonds while tears streamed down my face. I created the same mourning ritual when William Day's mother drove into an electric pylon and died. John said the pall bearers had to wear rubber gloves to stop themselves from being electrocuted. For a long time afterwards we used to laugh about Mrs Day's shocking death. My mourning rituals also included the many burials I conducted in the flowerbeds after my father gave John a pellet gun. John and his friend George would roam around the bush looking for things to shoot. Sometimes, George's sister Shareen would come over and we'd play a bit of tennis and then go shooting together. Shareen and I shot at an old golden syrup tin; John and George shot birds and frogs. It became a sore point between us. I was always having to bury the things they killed. I laid the poor dead birds with their wobbly heads into the ground. I poured some petal medicine on the blood oozing through their feathers and said a little prayer. I made crosses out of palm tree leaves to mark the spots where they were buried, and then went off into the bush to cry.

As I grew older I dealt with losing people and animals by singing the hymns I heard at school. I copied Annie Mackay, a girl in my class who stood up in assembly and sang about Jesus on the cross and how he suffered because of us and our sins. She sang about his wounds and his crown of thorns, and his sorrow. Her voice wobbled as she sang and the hymn sheet wobbled in her hands. I would look at the Christ thorn tree near the servants' quarters and run my fingers along its big white thorns that looked like shark's teeth. I hid away in the bush and did my best to sing my mournful songs in the same warbling way that Annie did.

***

Tennis tournaments in the holidays gave me and John a chance to stay with other families. We loved staying with the Frobishers who lived in Salisbury. The Frobishers had a swimming pool as well as a tennis court. There was a thatched summer house next to the tennis court where Professor Frobisher, known as Scrumpy by his wife, kept a polished brass trumpet from his military days. When their son Quentin, known as Squibs, wanted to summon the servants to bring us some refreshments, he got the trumpet and blew it. Their pool had a bar in the middle of it where Professor and Mrs Frobisher entertained their friends on the weekends. Gwendolyn Frobisher drove us to the tennis tournament every morning in her red Ford Capri which had rounded windows in the back. John and I pretended we were in an aeroplane. Squibs, sitting next to his mother, was the co-pilot. John and I sat in the back and sipped our imaginary drinks and puffed on our imaginary cigarettes.

I met up again with Professor and Mrs Frobisher in 1986 when I lived in London. I asked them what happened to Dolly and Sixpence who used to wait on us when we stayed with them. Mrs Frobisher said that Sixpence worked for them for nearly fifty years. Their servants had continued to look after the Frobisher's house post-Independence, after they'd taken Squibs with them to live in the UK. I remember that Sixpence was always immaculate in his starched white trousers and scarlet jacket. The jacket was edged with gold braid and he wore a red hat like a fez. The gold tassel on the top was the same as the gold tassel on the end of the bell in the dining room that Mrs Frobisher used to pull to summon one or other of the servants. Mrs Frobisher said that they'd decided the time had come for Sixpence to retire. They flew the 'old boy' to Cape Town for a holiday in the family jet. She said they'd decided to give Sixpence a sum of money rather than cattle at a farewell barbeque, and then they had flown him back to Harare. Mrs Frobisher laughed and said that Sixpence drank so much at his homecoming that he keeled over and died of a heart attack. I remember telling my parents the story and my father said "Once a muntu always a muntu."

***

I began to play tennis for long hours. The servants complained about the amount of time I was spending hitting balls against the back of their quarters. My enthusiasm was fired because I overheard the Colonel saying to my mother that I was showing enough promise to play at Wimbledon. I lost countless balls in the bush and broke the kitchen window. After I was told to stop hitting balls against the servants' quarters, I took all the eggs out of the pantry. I threw the eggs, one after the other, against the wall. John tried to stop me so I made him stand up against the wall. My mother heard us fighting and caught me squashing the last remaining egg on his head. She persuaded my father to get the Public Works Department to fix up the old clay tennis court. At first John was as enthusiastic about playing tennis as I was and we began to spend hours playing games against each other and practising our shots.

It became a sore point, however, when John began to use the tennis court as a landing strip for his model aeroplane. He and my father carried the plane and a flagon of fuel onto the court. There they filled up its tank with evil smelling petrol. My father twiddled the propeller around with care while John stood clutching the end of a long rope. My father knelt and braced himself, making sure not to have his fingers reduced to mince-meat in its whirling propeller. They waited for its horrible racket to reach fever pitch, before my father leapt to one side and the plane raced off at the end of its rope. John whirled himself around keeping his eyes fixed on the screeching thing, watching for it to lift itself off the ground. It rose magnificently into the air and John became a whirling dervish as it roared above the ground. It didn't take long before it spun out of control and crashed, gouging holes along the surface of my beloved tennis court as it ground itself to a halt. What made me fume was that my father never came to watch us play tennis. He never took me to my lessons with the Colonel, never came to see me play in a tournament and never walked around the side of the house to watch me and John in action.

John gradually became less and less enthusiastic about playing tennis with me. I showed him no mercy when he said he'd had enough and begged to stop. I remember his look of resignation on those hot afternoons when he threw his racquet to one side, and walked stoically over to the spot I'd assigned him at the net. When I had hit him three times at point blank range he sauntered off into the coolness of the house while I continued to batter balls against the wire fence. My mother took pity on John and got the Public Works Department to build a practice wall along one end of the court. Now I smashed my way through one hot afternoon after another. As I began to win more tournaments, I got a sponsorship deal with

Maxply. My mother collected my new racquets from the sports department in Miekles and brought them home in thick plastic covers that smelled of varnish.

When I had a tennis match to play, I slept with my right arm in a fixed position so that it wouldn't be stiff in the morning. I said prayers before I got into bed and prayers before I walked onto a tennis court. I said prayers when I touched the gold St. Christopher around my neck that Roseanna Baxter gave me. I gave my St. Christopher a salty lick before delivering a serve which needed to be an ace, and I did so when I was about to lose. When my father got in from work and heard that I'd won, he'd say "good old Champie". Eventually he just called me 'Champ'. I couldn't bare losing when I did and tried my utmost not to show it. I remember slamming every door in the house after I lost a match to my arch rival Belinda Jenkins.

I look at an old photograph of the servants sitting on the grass behind the kitchen polishing my tennis trophies, along with my mother's silver cutlery. I remember how carefully they lined my gleaming cups back up in the lounge when they'd finished. I remember how I could see my face, strangely distorted in the biggest ones when I turned them around to read my name engraved on the back.

21

In the summer of 1968 my parents took us on a month's holiday to South Africa. We stayed in the Oyster Box Hotel at Umhlanga Rocks, near Pietermaritzburg where my parents had met during the war. My parents' room had a balcony which overlooked the sea, while John and I shared a bungalow in the gardens at the back of the hotel. Monique had a bungalow to herself. There was a tennis court next to ours but we just wanted to be on the beach. I couldn't wait to wear my new bikini. The sea was a stone's throw away and we couldn't wait to run down to the beach every morning. The roar of waves crashing onto the rocks called to us, whether we were inside the hotel, or behind it. We breathed in the salty air and listened to the seagulls shrieking above the roar of the waves. We stepped onto the golden sand and marvelled at the brilliant blue of the sea. My father did his best to hold onto me and John as we tiptoed into the sizzling foam, only to be knocked sideways by the force of the waves pounding onto the shore. My father gave up and went to lie on his towel next to the swimming pool. My mother was nowhere to be seen. She and Monique linked up with Libby, an old nursing friend from her time in South Africa. The only time I remember my mother being with us was when a parrot bit her at the bird sanctuary we visited one afternoon with Libby.

The hotel dining room overlooked a swimming pool that was shaped like a kidney dish. Our Indian waiter wore a vermillion outfit and served our meals with a fork and spoon held delicately between two fingers. He spooned our food off his silver tray while the tassel on his vermillion hat swung like a pendulum over his nose. His name badge read 'Ghandi'; my father called him 'candy'.

In the evenings after supper, John and I ran off to play a game called 'dare devils' on the beach. The tide was coming in and the furious sea ate large chunks out of the sandy cliffs below the hotel garden. We ran in front of the incoming waves and waited until the last minute before leaping up onto a sandy cliff. If we didn't make it in time we risked being swept out to sea. There wasn't a soul on the beach except us, and we played until the thrill of launching ourselves up the sandy cliffs wore us out. I look back at those wild evenings and wonder what would have happened if one of us had slipped and been swept away. The cries of the one would have been drowned in the thunder of the incoming tide long before the other had run inside to get help.

***

The following summer my parents took me and John on holiday to the Victoria Falls. Their friends Paul and Betty came along, with their son Daniel. We stayed in the magnificent Victoria Falls Hotel and our rooms overlooked the famous "smoke that thunders" in the distance. We walked past the statue of Dr David Livingstone to go and look at the Devil's Cataract and to walk along the winding path with its tropical vegetation and beautiful dancing butterflies next to the Falls. At the Devil's Cataract Betty shook her head as we stood and watched the iron-coloured torrents pulverise their way into the chasm below us. "Who in their right mind would go over that in a barrel?" she shouted in my ear. I looked where she pointed and my heart stood still with terror. For years afterwards I had a recurring nightmare about the Devil's Cataract. The dream would always begin with me swimming in a lazy river, oblivious of my whereabouts. I would float towards an island up ahead. Too late, I'd see the spray beyond it and realise that it was the rocky ledge above the Devil's Cataract. I knew that I was about to be swept over the Victoria Falls to my death. I would jerk awake just before the inevitable happened.

22

John and I used to race our bikes endlessly up and down the long driveway to the big house. One afternoon John had a hideous accident and had to be rushed to hospital.

He wrote: *"I cut my leg open when I was in Form One. I must have been around twelve or thirteen. It was Shareen who rode in front of me – we were playing with her and her brother. The accident wasn't her fault - nor anyone else's. The consequences could have been dire for me but thankfully weren't."* The brake on John's bike impaled itself in the top of his thigh and ripped his leg open in a spectacular way. I remember looking in shock at a big black blood vessel throbbing at the bottom of the wound and feeling sick. My mother rushed him to hospital and he came home with the gash closed up by thousands of little black stitches. John said the doctor told him that just a millimetre either way and he would have bled to death. I used to look at the fat scar on his leg with awe. I felt grateful when he wrote and told me that it hadn't been my fault.

Monique remembered the accident too: *"As John says we all got hammered at various times and the only clear memory of a specific incident that I have is when John cut his leg and was in so much pain and Norman told him if he didn't stop crying he'd give him something to cry about – I've never forgotten how cross I was and it still makes me feel sad."*

The beatings were unrelenting and it's been sad to remember how often my father lashed out at us. John wrote: *"Cait we got smacked fairly often, which was 'normal' in those days. You frequently set me up for it! I remember crying about something – Norman gave me a smash on the bottom and said 'that'll give you something to cry about' The worst incident was when you chucked a mud ball at me. I was running and by a complete fluke you hit me. Luckily it hit me on the side of my head and missed my eye. Kids do these things. Do you remember when we threw squibs at Shareen? If any of those had hit her in the face she could have been blinded or disfigured. Thankfully they didn't!"*

I remember that time I hit him in the face with that mud-ball. I also remember how John graciously told my parents that he'd accidentally run into a tree. The time he fell over the bridge at the bottom of the drive and gashed his head open was the worst.

He wrote: "*You didn't push me off the little bridge – I fell off because I was showing off. I remember holding my feet and arms in the air and leaning the bike against the bridge and shouting "look at me". With nothing to support the bike it toppled over and I fell over the bridge. I didn't hurt myself badly.*"

When we shared these memories, I felt sad that John regarded a wound that needed stitching and left a noticeable scar on his forehead as a minor injury. It was a substantial drop onto a solid concrete bottom, and he landed on his head with a horrible crunch. It was a relief to know that I wasn't responsible for that accident either.

We were relentlessly mean to one another. John told me I looked like a horse and whinnied to annoy me. I said he was retarded. He said I was a spastic and called me a knucklehead; I said he had 'takkie lips' and 'clenched hair'. He asked Monique if ironing his hair under a damp cloth might straighten it out. When he started to lose his hair at a young age I was sure I was the cause of that too.

Monique had pointy nails which she used to good effect to pinch us. On one occasion she kicked me on my ankle bone and broke her big toe. She swore at me for leaving my pubic hairs in the bath and on the soap, and she wouldn't use the bathroom until I had plucked them out and changed the towels.

Monique wrote: "*If anything I tried to ignore Elspeth and Norman for most of my teens and hoped they'd do the same to me as I wasn't good at anything particularly except talking to my friends and smoking a lot and having fun - I do remember once when I'd cut my head open from throwing rocks at the water cooler that Norman didn't think I should take anymore codeine even though I had a dreadful headache.*"

I remember my father telling me that Monique had been brain damaged at birth. I also remembered a time when she'd had to have lots of tests at the Bulawayo General Hospital. When I asked her about this she wrote: "*I had a seizure caused by taking anorexine – was extremely naughty and careless at that age – wanted to be thinner and anorexine was an amphetamine that killed the appetite and gave one lots of energy. Of course, I never told anyone about that, but Jamie knew. So, I don't think I was brain damaged at birth nor was I epileptic; just didn't have the courage to own up to what I'd done! I had all kinds of EEG's and was never found to have any sign of epilepsy – the stupid things we do!*"

THE SECRET WORLD OF SHLOMO FINE

Looking back at our family life has been painful. Its turbulence played out, like the rumbling thunder that echoes and rolls long after its explosions have made you jump out of your skin.

Words like 'schizophrenic', 'manic-depressive', 'psychotic' and 'mad' have trailed along behind me like a turbulent wake. I relegated people with those names into an 'other' world where they scarcely counted as human beings at all.

***

Besides John's nasty gash and our visit to the Victoria Falls, we both remember 1969 as a momentous year. We remember my mother having to go into hospital to have surgery on her neck.

John wrote: *"She had a lump removed from her neck – the lump has a name which I can't recall. I think it was a goitre??"* When she came out of hospital, she showed us the delicate scar at the bottom of her throat. She remarked how grateful she was that her surgeon made the incision exactly on her necklace line so nobody would notice that she'd had her throat cut. I remember standing next to her in the garden one day and we watched a flock of birds flying in an arrow formation. My mother looked at them and said: "Just before I was put under the anaesthetic, I looked out of the window. I saw a flock of birds, just like that," she said, "and I wondered if that was the last thing I would ever see." She looked at me and said: "It's easy to die, you know Cait!" I remember the ground under my feet wobbled and the scar just below her Adam's apple took on a new significance.

***

When she'd fully recovered from the operation, my mother took Monique with her to visit Lesley in the UK. They were away for over a month. Lesley was considered the brain box in the family and my parents spoke of her with respect. What Monique lacked in brains she made up for with her stunning good looks, her hot pants outfits and her beehive hair style. I hovered between them in a private no man's land. Playing tennis was what gave me a sense of identity.

My mother and Monique began their trip with a visit to Penny who still lived next door to my mother's old family home. Lesley met them there and they spent a week travelling around the north of England. Then Monique accompanied my mother to meet some old friends from her nursing days. They travelled to Switzerland, followed by stays at Lake Como and then in the Lebanon. They returned with photographs of Lesley with her boyfriend. My eldest sister looked a lot like Carol King, leaning against a wall, smoking a cigarette and wearing black rimmed glasses. My mother brought me back a Swiss tennis cap for my birthday. She said it made me look like Suzanne Lenglen. I never wore it because it was a size too small for me.

While they were abroad my father diagnosed me with an attack of acute appendicitis. I was speedily admitted to the Mater Dei Hospital to have my appendix removed. The thing I remember most was being given a pre-med capsule to swallow by one of the nuns. She said it would make me feel drowsy before they took me to the operating theatre. I had never swallowed a pill before and I bit it in half. The medicine inside it was so foul that I almost threw up.

I spent three weeks in the Mater Dei being nursed back to health by the nuns. My father brought John along to visit and numerous of my mother's friends came by with magazines and games to keep me occupied. I came out of hospital a few days before my mother and Monique got home. It wasn't long before John and I resumed our mud-ball fights and our skirmishes on the tennis court.

23

One sweltering weekend, Monique's best friend Bethany O'Malley invited me and John over for a swim. Bethany lived in Famona, within walking distance of Ingutsheni and her parents said we could go over to her house and swim whether Bethany was there or not. So we tucked our swimming things under our arms and ran through the bush, over the burning soil, as fast as our legs could carry us with a joy that is hard to describe. The O'Malley's house was just a couple of streets away from the hospital grounds and all the kids in the neighbourhood had an open invitation to swim there. Bethany's mother ran the local riding school and Mr O'Malley liked to tinker with his car.

Gone were the days of wanting to jump in the fish pond or running around under the garden sprinkler to cool off. Gone were the weekends of being stuck in the house with nothing to do except play tennis or ride our bikes. We swam in the O'Malley's pool for hours and hours and hours. We ran back home bedraggled and tired, our eyes bright red and hazy from swimming underwater with them open.

***

When I wasn't at school or under water in the O'Malley's pool, I was playing tennis. Life became simple and pleasurable, and I fell in and out of love with various boys at tennis tournaments.

I danced long and slow one night with a dark-haired boy at a party who offered to drive me back to Ingutsheni. We stood and kissed in the moonlight and I showed him the Queen of the Night which grew near the car port. Its multitude of white petals glowed, pale and ethereal, and for months afterwards, when I looked at that beautiful flower, I pined after that boy like a dog without a bone. He never invited me out or spoke to me again. I've always wondered if his parents were cross that he'd fallen in love with a girl who lived at the local lunatic asylum. I found being close to boys a sticky and awkward business. I was so easily lost for words. I wished I was more like Monique. My mother often asked why I couldn't 'just be happy' like Monique or John.

***

Monique met Jamie Carrington shortly before her 21ˢᵗ birthday. John and I were not invited to her 21ˢᵗ birthday party which took place one hot summer evening towards the end of 1970. We climbed out of my bedroom window so that we could spy on Monique and her new boyfriend. It was with a certain amount of satisfaction that I watched Jamie and some of his friends take a communal piss on my mother's rose bushes next to the fish pond. Jamie himself pissed into the water whilst he intoned the words "dominus rectum" in a loud and serious way. I watched Monique stride over to reprimand him. "The Mother Superior's not going to catch me is she?" Jamie laughed in a high-pitched cackle.

Much to my father's chagrin, Jamie became a regular visitor. My father said that Jamie had a drink problem and that he was a cradle snatcher. Jamie had recently divorced, had grown up kids and was substantially older than Monique. However, I fully understood Monique's enthusiasm. Jamie worked as a disc jockey and dressed in fashionable clothes. He wore chunky gold jewellery which dangled down his unbuttoned shirt front and he wore a gold signet ring on his little finger. To me, Jamie Carrington was a freckled version of Warren Beatty and he dressed as suavely as Roger Moore and Sean Connery. Jamie drank like a fish wherever and whenever he liked because he had an African driver named Robinson. Jamie gave Robinson a grey uniform with a peaked cap, like the uniform worn by Lady Penelope's chauffeur in the Thunderbirds. Robinson acted not only as Jamie's driver but as a sort of batman. Robinson wore the same generous amount of Brut deodorant as Jamie did. Robinson kept a cigar clipper in his top pocket so that he could clip the end of Jamie's cigars for him. Jamie said that Robinson was 'the best dressed and best smelling zot in Rhodesia'.

I was thrilled to bits when Jamie invited me to play squash with him at the Parkview Sports Club. I wasn't able to win more than a few points but I didn't care. Afterwards I sat next to him and Monique at the bar while they sipped their drinks, smoked their cigars and introduced me to Bulawayo's other 'beautiful people'.

In 1973 Jamie developed a cancerous growth on his tongue and he was subjected to a lengthy course of treatment. I cringed at the thought of him having to have radium needles inserted into his tongue. Monique spent every spare moment at his bedside in the hospital. Cigars were banned for a long time afterwards and he went on to make a full recovery. From that point onwards he and Monique became inseparable.

The 'mother superior' developed a soft spot for Jamie which lasted for the rest of her life.

24

My father turned sixty on 2nd November 1971 and had to retire from government service. Towards the end of 1970, my parents had bought a house in Suburbs, a short bicycle ride away from the city centre, and the Bulawayo Centenary Park. The house was in a dilapidated state. It had a large derelict garden and a disused swimming pool full of emerald green water. My mother set about transforming it from a three bed-roomed house with a veranda, into a spacious four bed-roomed home with an inner courtyard garden, a television room, a new kitchen, a breakfast room and a self-contained annexe for Monique and myself. The swimming pool was emptied, re-cemented and given a new surround of crazy paving. The garden was landscaped. The wide veranda at the front was retiled and its sides filled in with flowery breeze block walls.

We moved away from Ingutsheni on 1st October 1971, not long before I wrote my O Levels. How springy the new olive green carpets felt underfoot in the lounge, and in the entrance hall, and in the formal dining room. I had a new iron bed with gold knobs on either end. Monique and I shared a bathroom of our own and her bedroom had an outside door. The whole wing was decorated in shades of pink, white, black and turquoise. Moving away from Ingutsheni opened up a whole new world for all of us. It was amazing to be able to ride my bike over to the park and visit the Natural History Museum. I spent many happy hours there admiring its collection of taxidermy-ed wild animals and its displays of African butterflies. I could ride my bike to school. There were street lights outside my window and class mates around the corner. We lived a few blocks away from my mother's best friend Betty. Betty had been knocked over by a car and had spent many months in the Bulawayo General Hospital recovering from her injuries. My mother looked after Betty's son Daniel who was the same age as John. The two boys became close friends. While I played tennis on Saturday afternoons, my mother and John went over to Betty's house. John and Daniel played and swam in their pool while my mother sat on the veranda and gossiped with her friend.

***

The part of the house which remained untouched was the servants' 'khaya'. The mains switch for the khaya was in our kitchen. One evening John and I took turns at flicking the light switch on and off. John said it was disco time for our two servants, Moses and Martha. Moses came and shouted at us. He said that he was going to join the liberation struggle. He said he would come back one day and kill us. I don't know what became of Moses but one of the boys who joined my Sixth Form was killed during the Rhodesian war. The servants' two tiny rooms were next to a triple car shelter at the back of the house. My mother drove her Citroen up a paved driveway round the back of the house to the kitchen where the servants unloaded her shopping bags.

Monique had been given a pale blue Anglia for her 21st birthday. She was able to park her car in the car port, and then let herself in and out of her private annexe without disturbing the rest of us. When I got my licence in 1972, I was allowed to use her car to go and buy her an ice cream from the Eskimo Hut ice cream parlour near the Bulawayo Fair Grounds. Monique gave me enough money for a tub each of vanilla ice cream with chocolate sauce. John was always game to come with me, and held Monique's ice cream on the way back. There she lay like a mermaid sizzling in the sun, spooning her newly delivered ice cream into her mouth with a little wooden spatula. John and I fell into the clear blue water of the pool, and swam, and sunbathed, and swam some more, until Martha rang the bell for supper. My father went into private practice in a block of offices near the Bulawayo Public Library. Now everyone, except my mother, lay in a row on sun beds around the swimming pool on the weekends, roasting underneath the sun.

25

My father joined the Rotary Club in 1972 and offered to host an exchange student from America. Calvin Lewis came to stay. I fell head over heels in love with Calvin and we spent happy hours over at my friend Mattie's house, listening to Who's Next and perfecting the art of French kissing. Calvin gave me Arlo Guthrie's album Alice's Restaurant and we used to listen to it with the volume turned up so loud that we could just about hear the words underwater in the swimming pool.

The first track on Alice's Restaurant is a protest song against the draft. It's a satirical song about a boy who goes along to be vetted for military service in Vietnam, and has to see a psychiatrist. He's an all-American kid from New York and the lyrics tell a sardonic story. Having spent the previous night drinking to work up some courage, the boy complies with the vetting procedure until he and the psychiatrist end up jumping up and down, yelling "Kill! Kill!" The recruiting officer, duly impressed, pins a medal on the boy's shirt and declares him 'the man for the job'. I remember my father coming home one day and switching Arlo Guthrie off, the needle on the record player making an ear-splitting screech and the album ruined forever.

When I came home from school the next day, I found that Calvin had gone and I never heard from him again.

***

Towards the end of 1972, my geography class went on an expedition to the Mushandike Study Centre. It was not far from the area where I had gone camping with Amelia and her family a few years previously. I had a tremendous fight with my mother prior to our departure because I'd fallen in love with Freddie Compton at a tennis tournament in Salisbury. Freddie was to be in Bulawayo that weekend playing for his school team. I went off on the expedition with a heavy heart. There is a photograph of us girls having just arrived at the camp. I am standing to one side, glowering at the camera. However, my sourness was soon diverted by two game rangers who were to be our hosts for the week. They made the most of taking us giggling schoolgirls down pot-holes and caves infested with bats, spiders and droppings, to canoe on a lake rich in mud and fish eagles, and into the bush, armed with rifles, to track wild animals. I came home with stories of barbeques and sun downers, and rapturous feelings for Kev and Ollie. The escalating bush war did not feature on my radar at that time in my life.

Not long after I got back, my father told me that the school had been in touch with him to complain about my behaviour. He said that if it wasn't for him, I would have been expelled by the headmistress for being drunk and disorderly at the barbeque on the last night. In the aftermath, I took to my bed and told my mother that I felt so unwell that I couldn't face going to school. My father said I'd learned an important lesson about alcohol poisoning. I stayed off school for three months while I underwent a series of tests.

***

I recovered in time to play in the Rhodesian Junior Tennis Championships. I had been selected to play for the Under Eighteen squad before my fall from grace at the school expedition. The team travelled to Benoni by train where we were met by our host families. Cindy and I stayed with the Thompsons. They and their two little girls, aged around six and eight, came and watched all our matches. The younger one asked me for my autograph at the end of the week, even though we didn't win a single match. When I got home, I told my parents what lovely people I'd stayed with and asked if they might come and visit us in Bulawayo. My enthusiasm was met with stony silence, and I soon forgot about the Thompson's and the promises of hospitality that I had made.

I managed to get into the Rhodesian squad again in 1973. This time we flew to Cape Town and were met at the airport by our hosts, the van Niekerk's. Barbie and I stayed with them in a neighbourhood called Parow. It was a bit awkward because neither of us spoke a word of Afrikaans. I remember that one of their sons said I was 'mooi' and 'slim'. When we looked the words up in their Afrikaans dictionary, it turned out he thought I was pretty and clever, not nice and skinny. Our team fared even worse than we'd done in Benoni. We didn't win more than a couple of games against formidable opponents like Greer Stevens, Ilana Kloss, Brigitte Cuypers and

Linky Boshoff – all of whom later played at Wimbledon. Ilana Kloss later went on to become Billie-Jean King's life partner.

It was the first time I had been to Cape Town since 1959. Barbie's parents came to watch us play and took me with them on sight-seeing trips around Cape Town. As a teenager I was bowled over by the cable car ride up Table Mountain and thrilled by the ice-cold sea at Clifton. I raced across the burning white sand and plunged into water so cold that my toes and my head got instant freeze burn. I decided that I wanted to go and study at the University of Cape Town. My father was thrilled because Cape Town was his home town, and he'd studied medicine at UCT.

***

I began my degree in 1974. I met Hamish du Pont towards the end of my first year. We were both members of the university tennis team. The team went to the University of Potchefstroom to play in the Inter-Varsity Tennis Championships, and by the time we chugged our way back to Cape Town, I had learned to smoke Hamish's cigarettes and we went about arm in arm at all times. Ingutsheni was still very much at the fore of my conversations. I entertained him and everyone else in the team with stories about how the inmates ate all our Easter eggs and lined our tennis court with wavy lines.

I became a regular visitor at Hamish's house. I made a friend in my university residence who came from Bulawayo. Georgina was part-Lebanese and part-English. She was constantly asked to get off buses, remove herself from beaches, and to clarify her ethnicity. She was refused entry to shops, bars, toilets and restaurants. One day I noticed a large burn on the back of her hand. She said she'd stubbed her cigarette out on her skin to see how much pain she could tolerate.

26

In April 1975, during the spring vacation, Hamish borrowed a car and we drove along the Garden Route to visit my friend Melissa who was studying social work at Rhodes University in Grahamstown. I discovered that Melissa had spent time inside Ingutsheni as a trainee social worker.

Melissa wrote:

> *"My experience with Ingutsheni would have been around 1978-1980, so just pre-Independence. What I remember is that most people seemed to be on Largactil with its resulting tanned yellow skin look! I have a memory of a young woman walking down along the veranda and then lying down and lifting her dress .... So distressing. I was told that their primal urges are very strong and they engaged in sexual acts often. I think I possibly met with the super on one occasion to discuss a patient, and I think I was fairly impressed with the diagnosis and understanding of the patient (he was black and I think witchcraft was taken into account) but it was a very medical approach with medication playing a large part. My other experience was social: my friend Gillian worked there and she used to get us all involved every now and then on a Saturday night for the patients' social evening. We would pitch up in this hall and see epileptic patients with helmets on their heads, and be grabbed by patients who would drive us round the hall in a kind of dance. One patient insisted on tying our shoe laces. We found it a strange mix of humour and pathos and gut-wrenching compassion."*

Monique wrote:

> *"I remember how angry Norman was about Dr Villiers and the helmets he invented for those poor people with epilepsy. It wasn't even to do with it being barbaric that made him so cross. Norman was angry that Villiers was getting extra income because of those stupid helmets."*

***

In August 1975, I went to see a psychiatrist. My father insisted that I did so because I'd told him that I wasn't happy with the courses I'd chosen for my second year at UCT. I had won a prize for Latin in my first year, not because I was a genius but because I had already studied Latin for A Level; I was a year older than my peer group. The students in my class were Law students who were made to study Latin as a compulsory part of their degrees, and so the competition for excellence was zero. After I won that damned prize, the pressure to do well was killing me. My tutor suggested that I might find studying at Oxford or Cambridge more satisfying. I told my parents that I wanted to quit. Besides, I was spending most nights tucked up in bed with Hamish. He showed me how to tap the side of my cheek and make smoke rings float above our heads in post-coital bliss. The rest of the time I was playing tennis or swimming in the sea with Hamish at Muizenburg.

The psychiatrist was a congenial old man who wore tortoiseshell glasses and smoked a pipe. He agreed that I had considered my options carefully and that my plan to do a secretarial course was a sound one. I quit my degree on 12th September 1975. Monique collected me at the airport and I was thrilled to be back home in Suburbs, ready to begin studying at Speciss College as soon as possible. My father came home that evening and said that I had fucked up my life. His anger baffled me because I'd done as he suggested. He avoided me and took no interest in my secretarial course. I found my mother sobbing quietly in their bedroom and soon realised that I was the cause.

In the months that followed, I did everything I could to avoid my parents. I went to college in the morning, worked in the afternoons as a teacher's assistant and took a job as a waitress at the Holiday Inn in the evenings. I used my earnings to pay for the secretarial course myself. At the Athol Desmond Centre, where I worked every afternoon, I became friends with Anthony Malaso, the 'tea boy'. We talked about Shakespeare and I shared my thoughts with him about the Franco Zefferelli film of Romeo and Juliet that was showing in Bulawayo at the time. It never occurred to me that Anthony would never see the film because he was an African. He wrote me letters in English and I helped him with his grammar.

Shortly after my 21st birthday, I completed the course and gained a diploma in Shorthand and Secretarial Skills. My parents gave me a one way ticket to Cape Town as a birthday present. I got a job in the student affairs department at UCT and Hamish helped me find a flat. Anthony and I continued to exchange letters for a few months after I left. I hope he survived the Rhodesian war.

***

In April 1977, I flew to Bulawayo shortly before Monique and Jamie got married. A month later they emigrated from Rhodesia to live in Toronto. Later that year Steve Biko, a prominent anti-apartheid journalist in South Africa, was murdered. Many of the students I worked with at UCT were members of the National Union of South African Students (NUSAS), and were defiantly opposed to the apartheid regime. They were being placed under house arrest for speaking out against the nationalist government. I learned years later that the student who ran the radio station had been spying on members of NUSAS on behalf of the Bureau of State Security, otherwise known as BOSS. This explained some of the strange phone calls I used to get, where there was nobody at the end of the line. It makes me laugh because I was so politically naïve at that time in my life.

I wrote and asked Lesley if I could come and stay with her. I told her that I was thinking of training to become a tennis coach. On 10th July 1978 I flew to London and felt excited about making my first trip abroad. I hadn't seen Lesley for nearly thirteen years and I was thrilled to set foot on English soil. I travelled to York to meet my long lost sister. To my intense disappointment, I found that she and I had virtually nothing in common. I stayed with her for ten days and abandoned my ideas of being a tennis coach. I decided to go and stay with Monique and Jamie in Toronto while I decided what to do.

Monique was delighted to see me. I went with her on a business trip to Ottawa and loved seeing the colours of the fall for the first time. She and Jamie took me to see Niagara Falls because it had frozen over. I had never seen snow before, let alone lived in a sophisticated city like Toronto, where life went on like clockwork despite mountains of snow falling over night. Going for a walk on Christmas Eve when the temperature had plummeted to minus twenty-six was so bitterly cold that it felt almost surreal. I found some part-time work typing up a manuscript for a fledgling author.

99

Just before Christmas Lesley phoned to ask if I'd like to take over renting her flat while she went to Italy for a work contract. It was a tremendous opportunity so I agreed to take over her lease when I returned to the UK at the end of January. Hamish flew from Cape Town and we spent 1979 living in Lesley's flat. We managed to save up enough money to go travelling around Europe on an Inter-rail Pass for six weeks before Lesley's contract came to an end.

I followed Hamish back to Cape Town in January 1980. He got a job as a sales manager in Johannesburg and I trained as a typesetter, eventually working as a commercial artist in the printing industry. I revelled in the Market Theatre where actors like Winston Ntshona, John Kani, Yvonne Bryceland, Janet Suzman and Antony Sher introduced me to plays by Athol Fugard, stories from Herman Charles Bosman and satirical sketches by Pieter Dirk Uys. We joined a tennis club and soon settled down to life on the high veldt. In a curious way, I felt at home in Johannesburg where we rubbed shoulders with Africans who thronged to work in the city centre and in the mining industry.

27

Trawling through my mother's diaries one day, my attention was drawn to an entry on the 21st February 1980. I discovered something about Jamie that I'd not known before. Her entry said: "*Monique phoned – Mrs Carrington is sick and maybe dying – at last – so we've agreed to do various last things – poor madwoman.*"

I wrote and asked Monique about this and learned that the 'madwoman' was Jamie's mother – that she had been a long-term inmate at Ingutsheni. In a drunken rage, Mrs Carrington had grabbed a carving knife and threatened to kill Jamie's sister. The diary entry on the following day noted: "*Mrs C died in the night – Norman has done all Jamie asked.*" Monique told me that Jamie was familiar with Ingutsheni long before he met her. He had roamed the grounds of the hospital with the superintendent's son who was at Boarding School with him. The two boys would meet up in the holidays, and take their pellet guns with them to shoot guinea fowl while Jamie's aunt was visiting his mother in the hospital.

***

John remembers that my mother's health took a nose dive in 1980. He was living with my parents in the townhouse they bought when they sold our family home and moved away from Suburbs.

He wrote:

> "*I remember Elspeth's heart attack well. It happened one morning when we were living at Esperanza – the ambulance came and got her! I thought she was going to die – so did Norman; who called the ambulance. Dr Chambers took care of her, once she was admitted.*
>
> *Norman was upset, he didn't cry but he was obviously at a loss. I was at college at the time, so Norman and I spent more time together then than at any other time. We used to go to the hospital together, smoke and drink together – Martha did all the cooking and cleaning. I did the shopping. I used to take Martha home after she finished washing up.*
>
> *Then Elspeth had her breast removed. It took her a long time to get over that. It was at this time the war in Rhodesia was at its worst. I know Norman spoke to Mrs Appleton to get me into the police. He*

used Elspeth's poor health as an excuse. I was very grateful they did this."

I remember my mother writing to tell me how relieved she felt that John had a desk job in Bulawayo. Even so, John had a narrow escape when a police officer was cleaning his rifle in John's office and accidentally pulled the trigger. The blank fired directly at John's chest and hit the big metal shark's tooth that he still wears around his neck.

***

At the beginning of 1981, my parents announced that they were coming to Joburg to stay with us for a few days. My mother said they had an appointment at the Canadian Embassy in Pretoria. She said they had an interview concerning their application to emigrate to Toronto. This was the first I knew that there were plans for them to go and live in Toronto with Monique and Jamie. Their application was subject to my mother's health being vetted, together with their financial security. They duly arrived, armed with all the necessary documents.

During their visit, my mother told me that she'd had an abortion in Pretoria during the war. I didn't think to ask her whose baby it had been or where the abortion took place. I guess she was worried about me living with Hamish and not being married to him. It was illegal to have an abortion in South Africa in the 1980's and just as scandalous to have a baby out of wedlock.

A few weeks later, on the 6th April 1981 my parents received confirmation that they had been cleared for emigration to Canada with a right of abode to go and live in Toronto. They left Zimbabwe on 24th August 1981 and never returned to Africa.

***

Hamish and I married on 8th May 1984. On the morning of our wedding, I soaked in the bath over at a friend's house. After lunch, my bridesmaid Melissa and I got into our outfits and toasted each other with champagne. I wore a creamy cocktail dress made of lacy tiers and we sprinkled dried baby's breath blossoms in each other's hair. Melissa and I each carried a spray of salmon pink silk roses.

102

Hamish's cousin Monty got us to the church on time in his battered old Austin Healey. We had a joyful wedding, surrounded by members of Hamish's extended family. I walked down the aisle on Monty's arm, and a number of my school friends travelled to Joburg for the occasion. None of my family came and, as the years rolled by and my distance from them grew, I thought about them less often. My mother wrote me a weekly letter from Toronto and I religiously wrote back.

***

Hamish and I had been married for eighteen months when the South African authorities created a tri-cameral parliament to represent whites, coloureds and Indians. I wrote to Lesley and told her that I couldn't bear living in South Africa any longer. She wrote back and offered me shelter. So on 14th February 1986 I boarded an aeroplane and left South Africa behind me forever. At the eleventh hour Hamish was offered a transfer to his firm's London office. He quickly applied for a passport through his maternal grandfather and exactly eight weeks after I left, Hamish joined me at Lesley's flat. Neither of us could believe our sudden good fortune.

We moved to London and bought a flat a short walk away from Highgate village and the rolling green spaces of Hampstead Heath. In 1986, Thatcherism made buying an ex-council property with a minimal deposit an easy option. I got a job as a typesetter and joined the Anti-Apartheid Movement. I road my bike down to their offices in Camden to help with administrative jobs; I regularly picketed outside South Africa House on Trafalgar Square. We joined a tennis club and settled into life in North London.

***

In October 1987, my parents flew to London and stayed in a hotel near Euston station. Lesley and her husband joined us to celebrate her fortieth birthday, and John and his wife flew from Zambia to be with us for the occasion. It was the same evening that a hurricane decimated the south-east of England. Hampstead Heath looked as if a bomb had hit it. It would be the last time that Lesley, John and I would sit around a table with our parents and our respective partners.

103

Not long after my parents' visit, I received a tape-recorded message from Jamie. In it he talked about Monique's increasing sense of desperation about having my parents living with them in Toronto. He pleaded with me to do something to help. Shortly after receiving Jamie's tape I began to suffer from insomnia. The thought of my parents living in the spare room in our flat caused me emotional turmoil. I wrote countless letters to Monique and to my parents. I spent long periods lying in bed crying pitiful tears. I had a recurring nightmare in which I drove around London and heard my voice talking out of the car radio, advising me to go and see a psychiatrist. I finally went to my doctor and asked for help.

The first thing I said to my psychotherapist was that I didn't think I was intelligent enough to do psychotherapy but agreed to give it a try. Around our third session Arthur said that he thought that I had been abused. As I left his house I blacked out. I crashed onto the pavement and broke one of my front teeth. I stumbled back to his front door and he took me in while I phoned Hamish to come home from work because I felt so shaken.

So it was that in January 1990 the stream of letters between myself, my parents and my three siblings began to flow with a sense of urgency and intent - and I made my first efforts to understand them, myself and the experiences we shared.

I worked with Arthur until my daughter Delia was born in 1993.

PART TWO

Hath not a Jew eyes? Hath not a Jew hands, organs, dimensions, senses, affections, passions, fed with the same food, hurt with the same weapons, subject to the same diseases, healed by the same means, warmed and cooled by the same winter and summer, as a Christian is? If you prick us, do we not bleed? If you tickle us, do we not laugh? If you poison us, do we not die? And if you wrong us, shall we not revenge? If we are like you in the rest, we will resemble you in that. If a Jew wrong a Christian, what is his humility? Revenge. If a Christian wrong a Jew, what should his sufferance be by Christian example? Why revenge. The villainy you teach me I will execute.
Shylock in The Merchant of Venice

How can we blame her for what history has made of us?
Rita Goldberg

(top to bottom, left to right) My mother aged 6, 12, 23 and 26 at the Springfield
Military Hospital in 1942
My father aged 30, 35 and 42 soon after he started working at Ingutsheni
My mother in the garden at the superintendent's house in 1963
My parents in 1968 on the top lawn, with part of the rose garden and a pond
behind them

1

Towards the end of 1991 Hamish and I decided to move out of London. While we were packing up the contents of our flat, I put all the works of art I had made into a carrying case. I shoved it in the boot of my car and drove up to Hampstead Heath. I found a secluded spot and tipped the contents of the case in a pile on the ground. Then I took a match and set fire to the lot. When I'd finished, I kicked all the ashes about until there was not a trace of my turmoil left behind – or so I hoped. Moving away brought with it the excitement of having a garden and the River Thames within walking distance of our house.

I was exchanging regular letters with my parents when, in March 1992, Monique phoned to say that my mother was seriously ill in hospital and was not expected to live. I immediately flew to Toronto expecting the worst. Lesley arrived the next day and we took turns at visiting my mother in the hospital. My mother had been diagnosed with emphysema soon after we moved away from London. She had changed from the robust and energetic woman I knew to an emaciated person in a hospital bed, and it shocked me deeply. She was painfully frail and woefully short of breath. She was clearly unhappy about her lack of privacy and her bed looked so cold and clinical that it broke my heart. I went and bought her a teddy bear to keep her company. I bought her a copy of The Velveteen Rabbit because I wanted her to know how much I loved her in case she just stopped breathing and passed away. It was an agonising time.

I stayed for five weeks and she got visibly stronger during the time that I was there. Not long after I flew back to England she refused to stay in hospital any longer. The hospital discharged her into the care of my father with a portable oxygen machine.

***

When I look through all the letters that she wrote me, I love seeing the bold and uniform script she used. It was sad to see the scrawl she sent me in the month or so before she died. My mother was generous in her memories and her letters gave me a strong sense of her early life and her background.

Letter dated 24th November 1990:

"When I was a small girl I used to walk with my Grandma, every Sunday, to put fresh flowers on the graves of my uncle, and grandpa. I still remember the awful smell of the old water in the vase as I emptied it, and refilled it for the new offering! I can remember too, thinking this was a silly thing to do, because two men would not appreciate flowers in such a smelly container – but I could only do as I was told, so very unwillingly I brought the vase back, filled with cold water to my Grandma, who put her flowers in, and plonked the vase back in the grave, until the next Sunday – and our visit! The grave was for my father's family only – my mother was cremated and it is just as well, she would have hated to be buried, especially with Emma Smythe, her mother-in-law, with whom she had nothing in common – there was no love lost between those two strong personalities."

I went to visit the family grave in Matson, Gloucestershire and imagined my mother having to trail along with her father and grandmother to the graves of her grandfather and uncle, just as she described in her letter. The church, St Katherine's, was over the road from a stately home called Matson House. I stood and looked at the grand house on the hill and I wondered whether my great-grandmother Emma had worked there as a domestic servant. The family headstone listed the births and deaths of Emma, my great-grandfather William Smythe and my grandfather Patrick's brother William Smythe. I got copies of their Death Certificates and noted that both William's had worked as porters at Gloucester railway station. They had both succumbed to tuberculosis just before the outbreak of the First World War, my great-uncle William at the age of twenty four. One of my mother's letters confirmed this.

Letter dated 30th October 1990:

"My mother was Irish in every typical way. Black hair, blue eyes, wonderful complexion, a great vitality and a free spirit. She was never a lover of domesticity and longed to travel which she did from very soon after my father's death, until her own some twenty years later.

Patrick Anthony Smythe (my father) was English, born in Gloucester. He had a brother who died young of TB which was rife in those days. His father William died of it too. My mother was as extravert as my father was introvert. He was a loving man, who sang songs when he was happy – to me – and read a lot, was interested in politics, wood working in his shed in the garden, made wonderful jams, marmalade, pickles, etc., smoked a pipe, had silver hair from age thirty. I only realized what a darling man I had for a father when I decided to become a nurse. He was so supportive of this career for me and helped to withstand my mother's violent opposition – and to stay with it and to prove to myself that I was capable of seeing it through to the end – and giving him that satisfaction – which was all he ever asked of me. He, like me, loved dogs and always had a devoted spaniel. He didn't earn much, but he was much loved by the men who worked with [him] and they respected him as I do – still."

Letter dated 29th November 1990:
"Senior was Basingstoke High School (for girls) as opposed to the Grammar School (for boys). The house in Basingstoke was 7 Penrith Road and I walked to school with my black dog Sam. "Crossway" was very different when Norman and I lived there. The houses on either side were not there. The land was my father's. We had a field to live in, with Crossway squarely in the middle, and the whole area was farmland where we walked and gathered holly for Christmas and mushrooms in Sept/Oct. My mother loved living there and had many animals – rabbits, goats, dogs, chickens, cats – one rabbit was a pet and hopped up the stairs and into bed with her! My mother was very interfering!! It never stopped and Norman really resented her on that score. He was always right in his opinion – so who was this old woman? It made my life, up until her death, very difficult and conflicted – but you were all such a source of happiness to me, that I don't remember being especially bothered by her. Although she thought I was a far too soft mother and not "in control" of you all!! No discipline!"

Before my mother went to train as a nurse, she worked as an au pair in Germany and had a brief romance. Like many young people at that time her boyfriend belonged to the Hitler youth.

Letter dated 24th November 1990:

"I've enclosed a photograph of the German family with whom I lived from 1935 - December 1936. Started at University College Hospital January 4th 1937 – a date I will never forget – my entry into the real world! My father died in, I think, 1943 – I was in Durban and mail was very difficult to receive – but I know he was fifty six years old – and I think he would have been buried in the family plot at Matson, a village near Gloucester."

There was no sign of Patrick Anthony at the family grave in Matson. I assume that my grandmother had his body cremated and his ashes scattered or perhaps interred in the churchyard at Old Basing where they'd spent their married life. I wondered whether the training at University College Hospital had other attractions - like free accommodation and a city like London to enjoy after her rural upbringing. How else did an only child get away from her parents in 1937 without being married? By all accounts, as her next letter suggests, there were issues with money at home.

Letter dated 14th March 1991:

"I, not Norman have a regard for money in terms of power – and honesty. I grew up being used by my mother as a messenger to debt collectors. She always sent ME to pay a bit off an account here, an account there – and I always felt ashamed. She also did a very bad thing to my father – she used me to take money from his account – he'd sold his mother's house on her death – and deposited an amount in his account. I still don't know for sure, but I suspect she forged his signature – and I was sent to collect the amounts she took. I was very young – maybe sixteen years old – but I knew enough to know this was wrong, because she ALWAYS warned me not to tell. I was too frightened of her to disobey but vowed in myself that I would NEVER do that to my husband, if I ever married! Then later, I marry Norman, who truly has no idea of how to manage money but has implicit faith in my ability to do – so when one is SO trusted – one cannot contemplate "cheating"! And one does try to be honest in monetary matters – even though one has a fertile imagination! Never mind – one thing Norman and I have never had problems with, is money."

By all accounts my grandmother Alice came from a middle-class family; her father, Chris Robertson, was an engineer. She and Patrick inherited "Crossway" when my great-grandparents passed away. I wondered if Patrick and his working-class background didn't quite live up to the lifestyle that my Granny Alice was accustomed to. On their marriage certificate, Patrick's occupation is listed as 'fitter and turner on the railways'. Could it be that when Patrick's mother died my grandmother felt entitled to help herself to some of her husband's inheritance, and used her daughter to do it? Looks like that's what she did. I'm not sure what happened to "Crossway" but assume that my grandmother used the proceeds from its sale to travel as widely as she did in the latter years of her life.

It's hard now to imagine how few opportunities there were in the 1930's and 1940's for women, until the war changed a lot of things. Universities were still bastions of male privilege and even the BBC discriminated against divorcees until after the Second World War. My mother often talked about the wounded airmen that she nursed in the Burns Unit at University College Hospital during the war. She said the men were known as 'guinea pigs' for the new skin grafting techniques that were used to help them recover from horrific burns. She said they were the bravest men in the world.

Letter dated 19 November 1992:

> *"I was christened on Christmas Day 1916 in Old Basing Church. Confirmed in the Church of England in the Cathedral at Winchester by the Bishop, sometime in the summer of 1934. Dan Fischer and I married on 10th December 1940 in St Pancras Registry Office with all parents present as well as my friends Penny and Elizabeth. Norman and I married in Camberwell Registry Office on Saturday January 25th 1947."*

A photograph of my mother in her nurse's uniform is dated 'Springfield Military Hospital 1942' on the back. It was by chance that John discovered that our mother had been married before. He'd been looking for something in a drawer and came across my parents' Marriage Certificate. Expecting to see 'Elspeth Smythe' on it, he was surprised to see that she had been 'Elspeth Fischer' when she married Norman.

Letter 27th January 1991:

"Norman and I celebrated forty-four years of marriage on Friday. How we've survived each other, I don't know! But we're still able to discuss our respective opinions and more calmly than in the early years, when we were so convinced that the view that each held was the only correct one. Now we know that each is entitled to a view and they don't have to coincide. We do care very much for each other's wellbeing, and treat each other with respect and concern. In fact, we still love each other. You ask how we met – at work. I was the sister of the 'staff ward' and he came one day to talk with a sick sister on my ward, and there it was, love hit us, and we did not do anything apart, from then on. I had left Dan approximately eighteen months and Norman was just back from Abyssinia, as it was where he had been with an Air Force squadron as their Medical Officer. Neither of us had any reservations. We just were young and he was ready to have a wife. Unfortunately I was not free to be his wife then, but we waited until World War Two ended, and then we went to England. Dan divorced me and Norman and I married in London on January 25th 1947. You remember the 'Annual General' party we used to have? That was always near the 25th January and we celebrated our marriage at that party each year. It became a fixture in all our lives – the friends too!"

In 2015, twenty-five years after Dan Fischer's death, I was able to obtain a copy of his war record. I discovered that he had been posted to South Africa eight days after he and my mother were married. Dan left for a posting in Belgium on 4th June 1944 but my mother stayed behind. The time they'd spent in Durban was a lot longer than I had previously thought. Did Elspeth dread going to Europe with the war raging and bombs falling? Had she met my father and fallen out of love with her husband? Did Dan ask for a posting elsewhere because he discovered his wife was having an affair? The only thing my mother divulged about her first marriage was that she told Monique that Dan was too close to his mother for her liking. No matter how many times John or I asked her about her first marriage, my mother replied that it was a wartime marriage and a rush of blood to the head.

Letter dated 8th December 1990:

"Thank you for sending me Dan's obituary. Penny sent me one too. Dan was such a dynamic person, inventive, witty and kind – but, sadly, terribly moody – and that's why I wouldn't live with him. I'd grown up with constant drama – with my mother – and longed to live a gentle, quiet country life. Take care, dear child, and be happy."

Dan's obituary was in two mainstream newspapers when he died in 1990:

"Dan Fischer qualified as a doctor in 1936, and then joined the RAF Volunteer Reserve medical branch, and on the outbreak of the Second World War became a serving RAF medical officer. He was twice mentioned in despatches and achieved the rank of Squadron Leader. After the war he decided to specialise in general practice. John was a supportive colleague and took immense trouble with his patients. He was once called to Heathrow airport, where a Nigerian woman who spoke no English had arrived, having gone into labour during her flight. After delivery he oversaw her admission to hospital and arranged for the Nigerian Embassy to supply an interpreter and provide her with books."

One of Dan's children grew up to become an acclaimed British actor.

***

One day during a visit to London, my mother showed me where she had slept in the Underground station at Embankment during the Blitz and, not for the first time, despite knowing the horrors of World War Two I wished that Dan Fischer had never been posted to South Africa, and that she'd never met my father.

***

I've often wondered when my mother discovered that she was pregnant. She told me that she had stayed in a Catholic Nursing Home called Nazareth House in Pretoria. It was a home for unmarried mothers. Nazareth House was run by a Mrs Maynard. My mother always spoke fondly of this lady, with whom she had kept in touch after the war. In her battered old address book I saw that Mrs Maynard passed away in 1977 and my mother had written 'R.I.P.' underneath her crossed out name. I don't know whether the baby she

113

was carrying was my father's but I assume that it was. I didn't think to ask when she told me about it because it was such a surprise.

Letter dated 1st March 1991:

"You ask about how I felt about having an abortion. I still, to this day, feel sad when I think of it. However, there was no choice. I did not want a child at that time – my life was a mess. I had to leave the army nursing service before "my condition" became obvious so I followed Norman to Pretoria, and found a doctor in J'burg who was willing and able to perform abortions. So off I went and it was done. I didn't feel "guilty" – just SAD to say good-bye to this little victim of circumstance – and I still wonder what he (it was a male) would have become, had he been allowed to live?"

Abortion was illegal at the time that my mother was faced with this painful decision. The fact that she had to wait until she was four months pregnant meant that her baby was well formed. It's likely that the baby was dismembered during the procedure. This must have been a traumatic experience. Maybe Mrs Maynard took pity on her and that's why they stayed in touch for all those years. I don't have a problem about my mother's decision to have an abortion, and I believe that every woman has the right to terminate an unwanted pregnancy. The sooner the abortion is carried out the better for all concerned.

***

I got a copy of my grandfather Patrick's death certificate and found that, on 27th June 1943, he died of bowel cancer. I thought again about Dan being posted to Belgium in 1944 and my mother's decision to remain behind in South Africa. I considered her situation, being without a father while the world was at war, being a long way from home but in a country where bombs weren't falling, and I'm not the least bit surprised that she found sanctuary in my father's arms.

I will never know exactly when she did.

2

Amongst her letters and diaries, I found mention of Martha with whom my mother kept in touch when my parents emigrated to Canada. I found this odd, considering she had accused Martha of stealing from her and often mimicked the way that Martha spoke English. I guess the relationship between madam and servant was a complex one, given that so many African women helped European women run their immaculate homes and raise their immaculate children. My father often called Martha 'a stupid bladdy kaffir'. I remember one particularly sickening incident, when Martha burnt her hand whilst serving us our dinner and dropped the sizzling roasting dish on the table. My mother docked money off Martha's wage to have the table repaired and Martha wasn't taken to hospital to receive medical attention for the serious burn she suffered. I feel ashamed to recall that when my mother bought our servants their food rations, she dished out the same off-cuts to them as the meat she fed to her dogs. My parents made Martha redundant when they left Zimbabwe.

Letter dated 21st February 1991:

"[Norman] had such agony of mind trying to accept a "black" government. He is very obsessive, and was at that time, totally obsessed with fear and hate of Dr Ushiwokunze, the then Minister of Health. He has, of course, by now forgotten all of that – and the fact that he told me over and over, that we would not be able to travel anywhere now that the "blacks" had taken over."

***

There is one particular letter that my mother wrote, in which her memories began to shift. The letter is titled *'Thanks Giving Day'*, and she underlined the title twice for emphasis. The letter is about a journey she and my father made to see some of Monique and Jamie's friends from Rhodesia, who also lived in Toronto.

Letter dated 8th October 1990:

"The Low's are in the process of building their house and it stands in "The Matopos" of the Ontario Lake District! There are huge boulders and lichens, the Sugar Lake on whose shores the house –

not nearly completed – stands looked a dull grey and the colours of the surrounding forests looked even more stunning – BUT – it was cold – that awful cold that makes one shake. I was the most warmly dressed of all. Dan had <u>thin</u> cotton pants, Ross had a T shirt as did Monique – Jamie in shorts, no socks and a T shirt. We looked a miserable bunch. We lurched and stumbled into their house, slipping and sliding, Monique holding my hand – which, for some reason, made me totally stupid. Somehow we all made it to the half-finished house.

They have really wrought a miracle, these two, working only on weekends. They have, during the summer, got together a three bedroomed, two bath-roomed <u>house</u> – put the roof on, put windows and doors in – and they will continue on until it's too cold to work, even inside – then they will come back in the spring and continue on. The resemblance to the Matopos is uncanny – and during the time we were there – freezing and eating non-stop, we saw the rain sweep across in a great, grey curtain over the surface of the lake. Ross explained to me that in a few weeks' time they will be able to ski down from the house onto the lake, by then, frozen and have fun cross-country skiing – can you imagine? After we had eaten everything we had brought, we, by now decked out in the Low's clothes – Jamie in tasteful mauve cords and red pull-over – almost as one – arose – and said how splendid it had been to see them, the house, the lake et al – and dived out in the slippery path and struggled as quickly as we could – all hanging on to each other – so that we could – hopefully – thaw in the various cars. So, with sighs of relief we set off – and the Low's went back to clear up the mess we'd made.

The drive back was fairly uneventful. We drove in and out of rain squalls and the car warmed us up – and then we came to that horrid place on the road – an accident – not on our side of the road. A young boy was waving traffic on, a body covered by a red blanket lay in the road between two partially destroyed cars. People stood around – no police or ambulance yet – it was a very disturbing scene. However, we continued on, and soon came home. Jamie drove straight to our house. I asked them in for a drink to warm them up, but they declined – and I was glad for that – I was still so shaken by the accident. But Norman and I went in – switched off the air conditioner. I made

Norman a good stiff whisky and me a sherry and later had a bowl of soup, and went to bed to read.

I dreamt of the crash and I was floating above it, and trying to get down, to ask them how did they have a red blanket? In my nursing life a red blanket was a signal of an emergency – and how did those unfortunate people have a red blanket to wrap that body in? It still bothers me – it was probably just a co-incidence – but odd. So that was my Thanks Giving Sunday. Elspeth Smythe

If you are still reading by now – I'll not keep you much longer – we have just had an election in Ontario, and to my delight – and very few others – the N.D.P. have, for the first time WON!! So we have what most Canadians think of as a "Communist" Gov. In fact it is not at all – it's just Socialist and I'm pleased to say there are eleven women in the Cabinet and thirteen men. They have only been in for a week – so can't comment on performance yet.

Anyway – my dear Cait – thank you for being the caring daughter you are – and you know how much I love you – and always will. Elspeth. P.S. Be Happy!"

I have read my mother's *Thanks Giving* letter many times because I found her dream about floating over the accident disturbing. It made me think about accidents of birth, accidents of love and accidents of war.

***

By the time my mother died, the letters we exchanged revealed a woman who had found her marriage pretty frustrating.

Letter dated 22nd March 1991:

"Norman was too busy being the good doctor, to be concerned about my role as the mother of a family – he, as I've told you before – trusted me to "know the answers" and if I didn't, then I wasn't a "good mother" and should "grow up" myself – and that didn't do much for ME!

I don't think anyone has spoiled your special relationship with me – you are my "beloved child" even though you are a competent, articulate and attractive woman of thirty-five years – you are – to me – a special child."

Letter dated 2nd April 1991:

117

"You ask me what used to frustrate me when you were all small children? In a word – Norman – he always felt that we were under his control – or I FELT that – and whilst I resented this feeling – I had a need to please him – so I accepted criticism – even tho' I felt I didn't deserve it – and I was angry and resentful of it. All that stupidity of making everything tidy BEFORE he came home in the evening – made me frustrated – and I so wanted him to be a part of the daily life of us all – but he remained aloof and critical – so when he went to Salisbury every month for two days I felt like a bird flying free – and we had picnics and sat outside in the dark looking at stars and eating food which Norman didn't enjoy and we all did – and later in your lives I used to take us out for lunch when he was at his Rotary meetings – just to have that sense of choice and freedom. Individually – I didn't know what to do when Monique was a baby and didn't sleep – my instinct was to take her into our room and into my bed until she slept and put her back in her cot – but Norman didn't approve and told me I was spoiling her – I was too tired to care and did that any way until it dawned on me that she was just "lonely" so I moved her cot in with us and she slept all night very quickly! It was wonderful!!

Lesley was a cause of dissention between us too. Norman was very strict about punctuality and she used to forget to come in for lunch on time when she was at Junior School – she had friends around the neighbourhood, and came in late (in the holidays) to lunch – it upset me to see her punished so harshly – but I had to appear to agree – so that Norman and I presented a "united front" – and I agree with punctuality and think it's an attribute and should be emphasised in one's dealings with children – I just didn't approve of the punishment for forgetfulness at age 7/8 – it seemed excessive.

You used to upset me very much by running away – but you know that. You also used to upset me when you were older by asking me to help you with homework, and then crying because you couldn't remember dates! It seemed to me such an EMOTIONAL response to something which really only required "parrot" learning – but you were probably crying for another reason – one which I didn't guess at – otherwise I might have been less impatient with you. Poor children you all suffered – but so did I – and so did Norman. But I can still be angry that he claims to be so proud of you

– individually and collectively – when it seems to me that none of us ever managed, long ago, to do anything to please or earn praise from him. I think I've learned a lot about "acceptance" in my life – that one cannot expect another person to change unless that person truly sees a reason to change – and ONLY then will the change happen – in the meantime love must be unconditional and constant."

Letter dated 9th April 1991:

"I was impatient sometimes but that was because I felt that you, nor the others, paid attention to me. Norman was effective in enforcing discipline and I was not – and that made me feel ineffectual. But it's all a very long time ago, and you are all grown and leading your lives – as Norman and I are ours – we have mellowed towards one another's attitudes. Norman says he hoped very much that you – being such a bright child – would follow his steps and graduate from UCT – he had given up on John who did not want to attend university – and Monique he did not consider intelligent enough – but you were his bright hope – and I hope, explains his behaviour when you walked away from an academic career. I thought you would enjoy being at UCT – playing 1st team tennis – having friends with you – altho I hated the IDEA of sending children to be "educated" in South Africa when there was a good multi-racial university in Rhodesia. I remember saying this in Suburbs – and I was looked at, by you, John and Norman as though I'd lost my mind! But my political thinking was NOT popular with anyone – except Yvonne. She and I consoled each other and dumped all the Rhodesian Front thinkers into a pit – where they ended up."

Letter dated 24th November 1990:

"You say in your letter that you wanted my approval, so you tried to be like Monique. How strange this sounds to me. You never were like Monique, and I tried to encourage you to be different – I wanted you to be different. Monique was, as a teenager, very superficial – all "looks" – and I found that not very interesting, although I was quite astonished at how well she made herself look – she had great skill in the make-up dept. and I still have no idea from whom she inherited this talent. The only real asset she had was her hair – and

she, as you recall, spent much time in "curlers" to make her hair look very pretty and shiningly clean. I thought that by encouraging your talent for sports – tennis especially – I could help you see that "looks" alone were not enough. One should be able to achieve. I thought this would help your confidence in your abilities and you would be glad you had more to offer than just clever tricks with make-up. I see now that I did not succeed – and that's sad – but you are now your own person and all my mistakes of long ago are now history! It's such a pity that children are either not able to express their feelings verbally – or if they can – they are ignored by their parents, who, for all they love their children, can't bear to be told that they are on the "wrong road", and so don't listen. However, the mitigating factor is that parents, although they make mistakes, are usually acting out of a passionate love for the child, so they should be forgiven."

3

I look back at my African nannies and I creep back into the warmth of Mary's soft lap. I lean over and pick a dandelion clock and I am once more the child that I was. I wish that I had belonged to Mary yet again, but I know that this is just wishful thinking, and it can never be true about me or my relationship with my parents. I remember how I had wished my mother had found the courage to stay in England in 1969. I blamed myself for her decision to return because I'd been hospitalised. My mother never said that she regretted having me, even though there must have been times when she felt trapped. Her stiff upper lip gave her an aura of elegance and stoicism. I remember how she would come home every Friday from the hairdressers with her newly painted nails and her finely powdered face. Along with the groceries she bought a copy of Woman and Woman's Own for herself, and a copy of June and School Friend for me. I remember all the comics too – Caspar the Little Ghost, The Incredible Hulk and Dennis the Menace.

Her close relationship with Lesley and Monique was undeniable. They were her English daughters. My savage temper must have made me seem uncouth and difficult. Rejection is an emotional word; I've experienced it as a sinking feeling, a burning sensation that ate into my gullet and scorched my face. Its accumulated weight pulled me down; silent and heavy. Looking back at my mother's easy relationship with Lesley and Monique has felt like having to haul a lead anchor from somewhere deep and lonely and agonising. More often than not, when I've given it a heave, I found I could only shift it a few centimetres before being overwhelmed by something unfathomable. I remember how my mother and Monique turned into a pair of elegant, fun-loving sisters after Lesley left home. They went on shopping sprees together to buy clothes. I'd often come home to find them sprawled on my parents' bed, laughing and playing Spill and Spell in my parents' bedroom. They gave each other treats like manicures and facials at the local beauty parlour. They gossiped about people I didn't know.

***

I look back at myself aged around fourteen with a mud ball in one hand and my tennis racquet in the other. I see myself throw the mud ball high up into a clear blue sky and smash it into smithereens with a force that, for a moment, satisfied my rage. Then, as the red dust fell to the ground and evaporated into the shimmering air, this was not enough and I looked around for something else to smash. I hear again the sound of my swishing racquet while hot tears ran down my cheeks. I look back and see myself behead all the snap dragons in the big flower bed on the top lawn. I remember the satisfaction I felt as I stood back to admire my handiwork and noted that there was not a single one left standing.

4

When Monique summoned me to Toronto in the spring of 1992 to say my last farewells I imagined that my mother would not regain enough strength to leave the hospital. One day, after Lesley had flown home, I decided it was time for me to fly back to the UK. I went to the hospital to say goodbye to my mother. I didn't feel sad at all when I took the bus from the hospital back to Monique's apartment. Instead of going inside, I walked around the block to a children's playground. It was a bitterly cold day. I went and sat on a swing in the icy sunshine and swung myself as high as I could. I hoped that my mother would die soon and that I would finally be free.

***

My mother died towards the end of February 1993. I waited for Monique to summon me to Toronto for her funeral but nothing happened. I discovered that my mother had made it clear that she didn't want any fuss after her death, so there was no farewell ceremony to be had. I asked Monique to post her ashes to me and, a few weeks later, the postman brought them as a special delivery to my door. I put them in the cupboard under the stairs and forgot about them. I went to London once a week to talk to Arthur about my blossoming pregnancy and my hopes for the future.

My daughter was born at the beginning of October. When Delia was ten days old, I finally got round to scattering my mother's ashes in the River Thames. It was unseasonably cold that day and Hamish wore the baby inside his coat. I pushed the box of ashes along in the baby buggy, and we walked down the hill to the river. I took the plastic bag out of its black box and chose a spot that I would remember. As I leaned over the water's edge, a curious swan sailed over, thinking that I was scattering some bits of bread for it to eat. Hamish and I walked along the tow path once my little ceremony was over. I remember looking at the iridescent blue and green feathers on a mallard duck squatting nearby when the word "suicide" suddenly flashed into my mind. I wondered why on earth such a thought had popped into my head. As we walked back home, I thought about my father living on his own in Toronto but most of all I wished my mother had lived to see my new baby.

Something about the timing of her death made me feel uncomfortable. In her last letter she wrote:

"You say that we – all – keep insisting that you will come here "in the Spring" – my dear Cait – no-one is insisting on anything – it's just a pleasant thought – but we are all adults here – and know that you can only do what you can afford and are inclined to do, so don't worry about what we say – though none of us remembers saying that any-way! Poor Norman got caught in the tubing on the oxygen machine – the tubing was in his shoe, and he tried to unhook himself – in so doing – he lost his balance and fell, with a frightful THUD – on the kitchen floor! The only really <u>hard</u> floor in this apartment. However, apart from a bruise on his hand, and a stiff back-side, grazed elbow he was not hurt, just shaken. He is now quite better – sleeping well and not having to get up to use the 'loo' – so he's very happy with his life."

I wondered if my decision not to visit had disappointed her and dented her will to live. I trawled back through her letters and eventually asked Monique what she thought - if it was possible that our mother had committed suicide. Monique said that Elspeth had put everything in order before she died. There were only a few precious pieces of jewellery and a minimum of clothes left behind.

When I discussed my suspicions with Lesley and John, we discovered that my mother had phoned each of us in turn on the day that she died. I was the last one on her list. It was a Sunday afternoon, not long after lunch, when she phoned. I was newly pregnant and I remember that we spent quite a bit of time discussing names for the baby. During our conversation she warned me that there was a dark side to pregnancy. Her comment troubled me for a long time afterwards, as I struggled to come to terms with losing her and becoming a mother myself. I think she was more aware of herself and her situation than she conveyed in the letters she wrote me. I believe that the correspondence between us had opened a door into the past that was difficult for her to face. Perhaps she was beginning to see how much marrying my father had compromised her freedom. I wondered if she was warning me how hard it is to protect children from life and all its dangers. Maybe she worried for me and my child too.

Monique and I have come to accept that my mother reached a point where her ill health had become intolerable and she decided that the time had come to end her life.

Monique wrote:

"You say the shock of Mum's dying made your memory shut down. For me it seems the shock made it stay forever. I had come back from doing a show in Edmonton on the Thursday mid-afternoon and began setting up the one in Toronto immediately. Later that night I went to say hello [to our parents] and we decided that, since the show would be occupying all my time Friday Sat...etc.. until the Wednesday night, I'd go shopping on Friday and drop off whatever we were going to have for a nice dinner on the Tuesday night as it was on my way home - and Jamie would meet us there ... I bought veal and some yellow freesias as the weather was gloomy.

On the Sunday, at the gift show, it was extremely busy with a huge snow storm outside, and I was a bit ticked because everyone was going to the Boswell's for their son's engagement party which was at two in the afternoon - and there I was working again. As you know Elspeth was really weak having to have the oxygen all the time and was very thin but she was quite happy and I thought looking forward to veal in white wine sauce for dinner on Tuesday.

In those days we didn't have cell phones but fortunately the company always rented a phone for the shows otherwise it meant no-one could contact any of us all day. So when it rang around two o'clock someone else answered it and called Chris - who then came and quietly told me I should go to Sunnybrook as my Mum had died. At first I thought it was one of Jamie's jokes ... Then I phoned him back at the Boswell's and he said Norman had phoned Debbie because he couldn't reach either of us. Norman told Debbie he'd already called 911 - so presumably he went in the ambulance to Sunnybrook because that's where I eventually found him in his brown jacket after sitting in the snow on the Don Valley.

When I got there, I just left my car on the street in the snow because finding a space would have taken too long and I think I thought maybe she might still be alive, so was racing around to find out where she was ... When I did, they asked me to go and identify her.

She had her green dress, long strand of pearls and her ivory earrings and looked perfectly peaceful.... I've always wondered if she had saved enough pills to send her off peacefully having talked to Lesley and John in the morning and then you in the afternoon ... we'll never know."

5

When I was in my teens, I asked my father what made him decide to be a psychiatrist. He told me about an experiment he'd done during his training at the Maudsley Hospital. He had taken part in some research into the placebo effect. He said it had sparked an interest for him in the power of the mind.

When I was thirty-five and he was seventy-nine, my father wrote me the first of many letters. In 1990, for the first time in my life, I'd decided to write to him and asked him to tell me about his childhood.

His letter began:

"I was born in Cape Town as you know, the only boy in a family of three sisters who in retrospect I think rather resented me and the fact that I was the only one who went to University. I do know that after both my parents died not long after I qualified and was doing my first house job in Maritzburg they tended to sponge on me in a manner I could ill afford so that I cannot say my relationship with them became very happy and I was relieved to be able to live away from them.

My biggest weakness was my disinterest in money and I could I think have been a much wealthier man than I am today but I have no regrets in this regard and never fail to be impressed with the way Elspeth manages our finances and how well we live. My biggest fright was the heart attack I had after we had settled down to live in Canada. It was awful and certainly put me off cigarettes permanently. My recollections of it cause me concern that Monique as well as John continue to smoke but it is not for me to try to interfere with their habits, even if I could.

I think you are a very lucky girl to have Hamish as a husband. He always has treated me with respect which I appreciate and he gives me a sense of security as far as his ability to maintain you and look after you. I want to wish you a very happy birthday and to thank you and Hamish for the financial assistance you give Elspeth and I now that we are living on our own which is a very great improvement to sharing Monique's apartment. I have found many of the tenants here of the same mind, many of them having lived with one or other of their children and then finding the independence of life away from them a great relief. I am very satisfied with the way all of you have turned out and it gives Elspeth and I great joy when we hear of Jamie's children as well as his sister's children and also see the fate of so many young people here in Toronto. Again, my dear daughter, I enjoyed writing to you and please give all my love and regards to your excellent husband – Norman."

I remember reading my father's letter to Hamish and saying that his attitude towards me made me feel more like a motor car than a human being. There was always a formality between me and my parents. When Lesley, Monique, John or I talk about them, we always call our parents 'Norman and Elspeth' – very seldom 'mum and dad' and never 'mummy and daddy'.

***

One day, in 1977, a woman with dark hair and a South African accent called at my flat. I remember a rather plump person standing in the corridor outside my door, with the view of Cape Town's mountains and palm trees behind her. She said she was my cousin Desiree. I must have looked blankly at her when she told me her mother's name because I had no idea who she was talking about. I don't remember how long she stayed or even whether I invited her in for a cup of tea. If I did report her visit to my parents, I don't remember either of them making an effort to explain how Desiree came to be my cousin. That fleeting moment is all I can recall. My father never talked about his family. I discovered years later that Desiree was, in fact, my Aunt Ruth's daughter. Her mother was the second child in my father's family.

Monique reminded me about another time when our Aunt Karin came to visit my father. She came to our house in Suburbs when she was in Bulawayo visiting her son Alex who lived in Khumalo, a largely Jewish suburb nearby. Monique remembered my mother coming to the door and telling Karin that my father was ill with the flu and wouldn't be able to get out of bed. Monique laughed and asked me if I remembered Alex or his two daughters who went to the same school as us. She said it was unbelievable that, when my father left Ingutsheni and started his private practice, he and his cousin Alex worked in the same building. Monique said that, as far as she knew, they never spoke to each other. My father mentioned Alex Liebenburg in one of his letters:

> *"There always was a great deal of friction between Alex and myself and for that matter [between] him and the medical profession in Bulawayo. Although one does not like speaking ill of the dead, Alex unfortunately was very money minded and as a practising gynaecologist tended to encourage his patients to have hysterectomies and for that matter abortions, regrettably not always on a sound medical basis."*

***

In 1990, in an effort to find out more about my father, I contacted the South African Broadcasting Corporation and put out an appeal for lost relatives. I remember the excitement I felt when I got a call from a man named Brian who turned out to be my first cousin. Brian is the son of my Aunt Ethel, the youngest child in my father's family. He told me my grandmother's name for the first time – Ruby. I asked if my grandfather's name was Mordechai and whether it was true that he had been a rabbi. Brian laughed and said that he wouldn't have called Mordechai a rabbi, more like a devout man who went to the synagogue often. He went on to tell me about my father's other two sisters, Karin the eldest, and Ruth the second child in the family. Ruth was in a nursing home and Karin was no longer alive. So, my father was the third child in his family - like me.

My excitement grew when, a few weeks later, I received my first letter from Brian's mother, my Aunt Ethel. She was delighted to have found me, having not heard from my father for over forty years. She begged me for my father's address in Toronto. I wrote back, my letter brimming with curiosity about the past and with a request for photographs of my father and his family that I had never seen. I sent her my father's contact details and waited in anticipation for her reply.

Her second letter was utterly different in tone. She told me that it was futile to re-open old wounds and that it was best to leave matters as they were. There were no photographs and I never heard from her again. My father thanked me for putting him back in touch with his sister. I'm not sure if he ever did reply to Ethel's letter. Maybe she'd sent him her phone number, hoping that he'd ring her up, and that's why her second letter to me was so cold.

I bombarded him with questions. He wrote back in his illegible writing on self-sealing aerogram letters. I pored over his scrawl in disbelief and my sense of frustration grew at how little he was prepared to share of himself:

"Of course as a healthy young man I had many girl-friends particularly when I was a young house surgeon at Greys Hospital in Pietermaritzburg and I sported a pair of tails and white waistcoat when we went dancing most Saturday nights. Monique was indeed one of my cherished girl-friends and you are quite right that in my romantic way I suggested the name for Monique to which Elspeth had no objection. All my love to Hamish and to you."

***

I tried to find more relatives and Brian put me in touch with Shelley, my Aunt Karin's granddaughter. Shelley was thrilled to be in touch and we exchanged many letters. She helped me understand much about my father's background but still there were no photographs.

Shelley wrote:

"Once upon a time Shlomo Fine was born in Vienna, Austria. Shlomo married and had two children, Ezra and Mordechai. Shlomo was born to a very wealthy family. He himself was a banker. It was his desire to go to Jerusalem to die. (This is the desire of every Jew and every year we traditionally say to one another "next year in Jerusalem"). He arrived in Jerusalem and settled in Mao Shoarim. This is a very, very religious part of Jerusalem. The people who live here are called "Chassidic Jews". They wear black dress and men have distinctive side burns. Women wear head coverings, etc, etc. Mordechai married Ruby Silverstein and the first of four children was born – Karin Fine (1902).

Now suddenly came the end of the Ottoman Empire in Palestine (i.e. Turkish rule). The Fine family lost all their money. Both Ezra and Mordechai decided to emigrate to South Africa. Mordechai decided to emigrate to Cape Town in 1906 with his wife Ruby and daughter Karin (then 3 years old). His brother Ezra settled in Johannesburg where he worked as a brush maker. There is/was a branch of the Fine family in Johannesburg.

Mordechai and Ruby settled in Cape Town. They died in 1937. Mordechai died on 19th December 1937 of a coronary thrombosis at the age of sixty four. Mordechai also worked as a brush maker. As I have already said, he was a respected member of the community and did a lot of work for the synagogue. The family were members of the Woodstock Synagogue. This was a respected end of town in those days. He gave his wife Ruby a hard time. I am not sure but I seem to remember hearing that her health was not good - Ruby died of diabetes mellitus and a coronary thrombosis on 17th February 1937 aged fifty seven.

Mordechai and Ruby's four children were: Karin – 1902-1981; Ruth – 1909; Shlomo – 4th November 1911; Ethel – 1920."

So, I learned that my father was, in fact, named after his grandfather. My father's birth certificate shows how he crossed out his Hebrew name, Shlomo and named himself 'Norman' in his own spidery handwriting. On it, his father Mordechai's occupation is listed as 'draper' and his address is given as 'Edward Street, Salt River, Cape Town'. On my parent's Marriage Certificate in 1947, my grandfather Mordechai's occupation is listed as 'estate agent'. Mordechai's occupation on his death certificate is listed as a 'general dealer'. Clearly my father fabricated a thing or two about his background when he married my mother.

During the course of researching my father's family history, I discovered that Ezra disembarked from a freight ship in Cape Town in 1905. His age was listed to be thirty nine. As Mordechai was sixty four in 1937 when he died, I worked out that Ezra was seven years older than his brother. Mordechai had followed his brother in 1906 with his young family and had set up home in Salt River. Mordechai Fine ran a hard ware store down the street from where my father had grown up. His son Shlomo attended Saks School and went on to study medicine at the University of Cape Town.

***

I got a copy of my father's academic record at the University of Cape Town where he began his studies in 1929. By this time my father's name was Norman Fine. I discovered that he failed his first year and struggled to get his degree. He achieved third grades for all his subjects, with the exception of surgery and medical jurisprudence, for which he got second class passes. I felt infuriated. I remembered his words when I asked him for a second chance, to go back and continue with my degree: "You've had your chance chum, so that's it. There's no going back."

6

I phoned my father every Sunday after my mother died, and when Delia was born, I wrote to him every week with news of her development. I sent him photographs of my adorable baby. After a few months of sleep deprivation, the euphoria of giving birth slowly wore off. I began to find it very difficult to cope. I wrote and told my father that I was struggling with exhaustion. My father wrote me a series of letters in his illegible handwriting.

Letter dated 25th December 1993:

"I am writing to you on this Christmas Day having just come from Monique where she gave me your most acceptable gift. I am keeping very well and am happy to be so lucky as to have the children I have and also to continue to enjoy my good health. I hear from Monique that Delia is making her presence heard. A very healthy pastime. I am so glad you and Hamish and Delia keep well and send you all my love - Dad"

Letter dated 29th December 1993:

"You are quite right about Elspeth and I and we certainly loved all our Xmas's at Ingutsheni with all Mum's lovely roses to help the festive scene until time as it does made them fade away."

Letter dated 30th January 1994:

"As I sit writing this letter I am looking at an enlarged photo of my first lovely granddaughter which Monique very kindly arranged to have mounted in a frame given to me by friends at Xmas. She is indeed a beautiful girl and I and you and Hamish must feel very very proud of her. I am glad to write that I continue to be fortunate in my health and my children. Monique in particular remains a tower of strength to me and helps me manage my life in all sorts of ways including a welcome invitation to their apartment for a very lovely and usually most excellent meal. Again all my love and thank you for giving me such a lovely granddaughter - Dad"

Letter dated 20th March 1994:

"I thought it would promote your return to good spirits if I sent you a menu from the Sweet Gallery, the restaurant which Monique, Jamie and I frequent when I want to give Monique a break from home cooking. I do hope you continue to regain your good spirits and that all goes well with the baby. I keep very well and continue to count my very good fortune in keeping as well as I feel and as well as my medical check-up reveals I am. I am deeply concerned about the situation in South Africa as our and yours too television coverage [sic] indicates the killing continues. I do hope you continue well. All my love - Dad."

One rainy Sunday afternoon when Hamish was out, in desperation I phoned my father. The rain was making little rivers down my study window and I told him that I had been diagnosed with post-natal depression. I remember listening to my father's heavy nasal breathing on the other end of the phone while I waited for him to say something. "Hell, man, Cait, you're not suicidal are you?" As soon as Hamish walked in the door, I shoved the baby into his arms and told him "You've got to look after the baby today. I can't go on." I stumbled out the door, climbed into my car and drove around for hours. Eventually I sped off down the M40 to London until I got to Hampstead Heath. I walked to the ponds where we used to swim in the summer. I didn't care about the rain and I felt so numb with exhaustion that I couldn't cry. All I could think about was dying. I knew that I needed help, but Hamish's company was struggling and we could not afford for me to work with Arthur any longer. By now Delia had started to cut some teeth and I couldn't stand it when she cried. One terrible day I shook her very hard and I realised that it silenced her in a way that frightened me. I never did it again. Another time, when I was feeding her, she began to cry and I screamed so loudly that my neighbour came running over to see what had happened.

My exhaustion mounted. One day I left Delia with Hamish and drove off to a nature reserve on the outskirts of Oxford. I walked around for hours. I sat and cried in the shade of a comforting tree and wondered what on earth I was going to do. Eventually I climbed up onto a rocky outcrop and looked out over the valley towards Oxford. As I looked at the beautiful buildings in the distance, I decided I wanted to live. I went home and found Hamish looking shaken and anxious. He took me to see an emergency doctor, whose stern and impassive face only made me feel ill with apprehension. He said that post-natal depression was a serious mental illness and suggested that a course of anti-depressants would do the job.

I went to see my doctor. He also suggested that a course of anti-depressants would help. Eventually Hamish's health insurance covered me to go and have therapy for two weeks in a Rudolf Steiner Clinic for terminally ill people. I agreed to go because I could take Delia with me. I had a massage every day, did some clay modelling, talked to a German clinician and ate vegan food. Someone came and took Delia away from me every evening at six, and I went and fetched her every morning. She was now nearly eight months old. I worried constantly that she was missing me and most likely screaming the place down out of my hearing as I trudged up to my room and crawled gratefully into bed.

I remember sitting in the sunshine with Delia in the garden there and thinking "So this must be what it felt like to be locked away in a strange place like Ingutsheni where nothing makes sense". One of the massage therapists said: "God never sets anyone a task that is too big". Now I wasn't only letting myself down, I was going to fail God as well. Followers of Rudolf Steiner entertain the belief that a child chooses its parents in order to pass certain tests in this life, before heading on out to the next life. Looking back on this bizarre episode in my life, it strikes me as completely ludicrous that I would have chosen my particular mother and father so that I might have the task of learning about insanity, at a place like Ingutsheni.

When I got home from the clinic, having to cope with my baby alone once more hit me very hard. I drove around aimlessly one Sunday, having left the baby with Hamish. I went to a hardware shop on my way home and bought a hose pipe and some clamps. I lay in the bath that night and sobbed. I told Hamish that I just couldn't cope with being a mother. He took me to see the same impassive doctor who immediately booked me an appointment at the Outpatients Department of the Warneford, the psychiatric hospital in Oxford. There I found myself talking to another impassive man, this time a psychiatrist. I assured him that I had not harmed myself or my child, that I wasn't really intent on committing suicide, that I was just exhausted and frightened by the responsibility of having a baby.

***

Hamish's brother and his wife came to visit. My sister-in-law suggested that it might be an idea for me to see a therapist that Hamish knew in London. Hamish took me and my baby to meet her, and she agreed to see me once a week. I drove to London every Monday and took Delia with me. While my baby slept outside her consulting room in her buggy, I told this woman that I had fallen in love with Delia from the moment I saw her but I didn't think I could cope long term. She suggested that if I really decided I couldn't be a parent, I could give Delia up for adoption. During this terrible time, whilst her words offered me a modicum of relief, they also added an edge to my despair that felt like a knife being twisted inside my gut. It was at that point that I finally agreed to try out some anti-depressants. I saw a consultant psychiatrist in Oxford who told me that many capable people were on anti-depressants, and that there was no need to feel ashamed for doing so. She assured me that I wouldn't be addicted to taking drugs for the rest of my life. I was still not convinced and broke the pills into quarters, so that I took one quarter in the morning and another at night.

It was Delia's crying in the middle of the night that I was struggling to cope with more than anything else. Hamish and I went to see a sleep therapist, who gave us details about a 'controlled crying' method. This required us to leave her to cry for increasingly long periods of time. On the first night I got so agitated after about half an hour that I pushed my husband out of the way and picked my baby up.

I never did get the hang of letting Delia cry at night. I simply took her to bed with me, and Hamish slept in her bedroom. We played musical beds until Delia simply grew out of wanting to be with either of us at night. Hamish proved heroic when the time came for me to wean her. He looked after Delia through the night, until she got used to being without the comfort of my breasts. I could not believe my good fortune in having such a wonderful little girl in my life.

***

On my daughter's first birthday I held a Naming Ceremony for her and threw my anti-depressant pills in the bin. A woman who'd been in my ante-natal class came to the Naming Ceremony and asked me if I'd share a nanny with her when she went back to work. Carol and her daughter Alexia became the best friends my daughter and I could possibly want, and so my new life began. I had two days off a week and I slowly regained my confidence, while Delia went and played with Alexia. Our house became a place where I revelled in the joy of getting to know other women in all the intimate and humorous ways that I'd never experienced before. I made many close friends and so did my little girl.

7

My relationship with my father grew closer and I started to share my feelings with him.

Letter dated 8th September 1994:

> *"I was delighted to have your letter and to hear your voice on the phone – my very new and sparkling telephone which Jamie found for me at the Bay. I am overjoyed to read of how much better you are feeling and I can appreciate that the stresses and strains of the past few months have placed such a strain on your relationship with Hamish. Please give him my love and all the best for his business future. I am glad you are getting some help and counsel from the lady you are seeing. We are all in need of help of this kind at some time or another. Elspeth was indeed a very wonderful but also insecure person and not inclined to be sociable. I know what a strain it was for her when I joined Rotary. I agree entirely with your comments about my job but I loved and enjoyed it. I do love you and look forward to the photographs. All love - Dad"*

I remember reading this letter and thinking that his description of my mother not being sociable was very odd indeed. She was always entertaining her friends, even when we lived at Ingutsheni. I guessed that Monique and Jamie were trying to get him to socialise with other people now that he was having to live on his own.

***

In 1994 Hamish and I went to Cape Town to show Delia off to his sister and various friends. I went to meet my cousin Shelley and, for the first time, I saw a photograph of my Aunt Karin. I noticed that Monique and my aunt bear a strong resemblance to each other. I visited the Jewish Cemetery in Salt River. There I found Ruby and Mordechai's headstones. My Jewish grandparents lie side by side underneath two enormous monoliths at least eight feet tall.

The headstones were mainly inscribed in Hebrew. I found someone to translate the inscriptions for me:

> *"An innocent/pure and honest woman / Ruby the daughter of Avraham Fine / Died in the 57th year / Zayin (9th) Adar Tartzaz – 5697 / May her soul rest in Peace"*

138

"In memory of our dear father / Mordechai the son of Arye Fine / Died on tet Vav (15th) Tevet Tarzach – 5698 / In the 62nd Year of his life / Mourned by his children and grandchildren and by the members of the Great Camp of Israel / May his soul rest in Peace".

Shelley explained the Hebrew wording as follows:

"According to the tombstone: Ruby is the daughter of Avraham. That is her Hebrew name. That is how it is written in Hebrew on the tombstone. This is how it is written: Ruby daughter Avraham. It does not include the family name itself. E.g. I don't call you Cait, daughter Norman Fine. I would call you Cait, daughter Norman."

At the time I found my grandparents graves, I had no idea that my father came from an Orthodox background. He never attended shul. He observed none of the Jewish holidays and followed none of the Jewish dietary laws.

Shelley explained the situation in which my father found himself:

"[Norman's] parents emigrated from Jerusalem before he was born. [His older sister] was born in a very religious area of Jerusalem. We are Jewish and it is a law (still observed to this day) that one may not marry out of the faith of Judaism. If a child marries a non-Jew the parents treat this as a tragedy - in fact the rituals are observed for the mourning of [the] death of a child. This is what happened with your father when he married your mom. He did not reject his parents - his [family] rejected him."

I remember my father's sayings: "No news is good news", "Things are bad", and "One must not speak ill of the dead". When I was having friendship problems he told me "to be sensibly selfish" and to cut myself from the person who was upsetting me.

When I consider my mother's abortion, my father transgressed many religious taboos: he committed adultery with a married woman, fathered an illegitimate child and helped his mistress have the pregnancy terminated. According to Jewish law, my father was not only dead, he was also a murderer. No wonder he avoided his three sisters and his extended family like the plague. No wonder he turned his back on his Jewish roots.

Letter dated 9th February 1994:

"Of course I had to return to my job as a young house doctor when my parents died so that I was unaware of any of the news you now give me about my parents' burial. No I had no parents over falling in love with anyone as at that time I was too busy as a student to have time for such frivolities. I don't mind your asking me these things one bit. I am delighted with my health and with you, Lesley, Monique and John."

I found my father's Freudian slip when he wrote: *"I had no parents over falling in love"* to be key in the trauma that he kept so carefully hidden. He lost first his mother and then his father in the same year, when he was twenty six. As the only son in his family, he was expected to take care of his sisters, to be strong and not fall apart. I think he did this very well in the immediate aftermath of their loss because his younger sister Ethel said in her first letter how wonderful he had been to her at the time. She was nine years younger than Norman and it must have been very hard for her at the age of seventeen to lose both parents in the same year.

My father didn't have any memory of the mighty headstones that I discovered in 1994, so perhaps his sisters and the Jewish community in Woodstock had had them erected. The war may have helped him escape some of the responsibilities he felt towards his sisters, but it got him into hot water when he fell in love with Elspeth.

It's also possible that my mother offered Norman a kind of respite from being Jewish. Jews were actively discriminated against in parts of South African society. They were barred from joining various clubs, prevented from working in certain organisations and they were called derogatory names like 'kikes', 'yids', 'chaimies', 'shnorras' and 'ghuttas' amongst others.

***

I had never seen a photograph of my paternal grandparents until a distant cousin got in touch with Brian and he sent her a photograph of Ruby and Mordechai. She, in turn, sent it to me. My Jewish grandparents are standing in front of their shop in Salt River. The photo isn't dated so I don't know how old they were at the time. John bears a strong resemblance to his Jewish grandfather. Lesley is the one who most closely resembles my mother with her beautiful wide eyes and the many years she has lived in England have provided her with a crisp English accent. I look very much like Norman.

***

When Delia was eighteen months old, Hamish and I flew to Toronto to show my father his first grandchild. By then Delia was an energetic little girl with blonde curls and deep blue eyes. She loved nothing better than to stand on a chair and sing her favourite nursery rhymes like a fog horn.

My father beamed at her and Delia beamed back at him.

8

On 13th August 1995 I got a phone call from Monique to say that Jamie had found my father lying dead on the bathroom floor in his apartment.

Monique wrote:

"*In the months before Norman died, you'll probably remember he had become increasingly paranoid about people stealing his blue box [a box for recycling waste] - not letting Naomi in to clean - all sorts of other strange things, including not washing well, and slicing and dicing his face when he shaved. I've always thought he knew his behaviour wasn't good, and the road he was on wasn't going to get any better, so decided the time had come and put the electric razor in the sink knowing it would give him a sufficient jolt to finish him off.*

You'll remember we came to you that Christmas and I think you were a little shocked when we told you our thoughts, but I really do believe he was so scared of dementia / Alzheimers - and the fact he was so alone - that he didn't want to carry on. His life wouldn't have got any better, that's for sure. We were always so scared for him, and had started to make inquiries into him moving into Baycrest, which is a facility for the elderly who can't manage any longer. I don't think he knew about that, but if he did, he wouldn't have wanted to go there.

During the week before he died, we both were busy setting up the gift show which means being out near the airport each day, eight to six-ish, so only saw him on the Tuesday night for dinner, knowing we were busy for the weekend at the show. Normally we'd go there, or he'd come here, some time over the weekend. I used to phone him each evening around six, just to chat, but when I phoned on the Friday night, he didn't answer. It wasn't the first time that had happened, so I wasn't concerned. He sometimes just went to bed at odd times. Saturday I phoned again - still no reply, but we were both at the show - but decided we'd go over there on Sunday when it closed, to make sure he was just being himself. When we were driving close to the building, I could see the lights were on in his flat, so felt so relieved that he must be OK. When we got to his door, I told Jamie to go - scared something had happened - so waited outside the open door. I think I knew he was dead actually. I'd been phoning from the show on and off all day and had told Sue, who also worked at the show, that we were going over there because something was wrong.

Jamie shouted to me not to come in. He closed the bathroom door, so I didn't see him, and called 911. Within a few minutes, these huge fire fighters arrived, followed by three policemen. They went into the bathroom, but didn't stay long - but told us Norman was dead, and the coroner had been called. After an hour or so, a man who said he was the coroner arrived and told us he'd died - but for the life of me, I really can't remember whether he said he'd had a heart attack. I think he did. Have to look at the death certificate to see what it says. [The death certificate does indeed say that Norman suffered a heart attack]. After a bit Debbie and Bert showed up, as well as an ambulance and the funeral service people who took Norman off to their mortuary. It was a long night!

By the time we left, I think we were so relieved that he hadn't suffered.

After Mum died, we'd tried everything to get Dad to be friends with someone in their building, but he was so strange that way - always so critical of others - and also his neighbour shouted at him about his radio being too loud all the time - remember how deaf he was - so he had no company except when we went over, or he came to us - not that it really seemed to bother him much - he loved his own company always, and enjoyed his radio, T.V and going shopping. He really never seemed dreadfully unhappy. After Mum died, I asked him if he wanted to come and stay for a bit, but he didn't, nor did he cry - he was really such a 'controlled' person - very sad."

***

One evening, like a vision in a smoke screen, I realised that my father had committed suicide. He contrived to make his death look like he had suffered a heart attack by filling the basin in his bathroom with water and holding his electric razor in one hand before swallowing his pills. He had taken an overdose and did a great job at disguising it. When I thought about how carefully my parents concealed their suicides I could see that their medical expertise was key. They knew

143

there would be legal implications if Monique or Jamie were aware that they were planning to take their own lives.

My father was there when my mother made her farewell phone calls, and when she swallowed her pills. It may explain why he didn't cry in the immediate aftermath of her death. I feel sure that's why suicide was on his mind when I told him that I was feeling depressed.

9

Monique posted my father's ashes to me and the friend who was looking after Delia that day, signed for them. I couldn't imagine scattering his ashes in the northern hemisphere. I put them away in the under-stairs cupboard until I decided what I was going to do with them.

On 26th March 1996, I flew to Zimbabwe and took Delia with me. Hamish was in the process of being made redundant and so I went on my own. I flew to Harare to stay with Melissa and then I took Delia to meet John who was still living in Zambia. My plan was to scatter my father's ashes on the top lawn of the big house at Ingutsheni. John declined my invitation to attend the ceremony at Ingutsheni. I hired a car and travelled down to Bulawayo where Delia and I checked into the Holiday Inn.

I drove to Ingutsheni the following morning. It was more than twenty years since I had been back, and it seemed like just the other day. I went to the little house first and took a photograph of it. I drove around the back of the hospital, past the women's ward, the laundry and the administrative offices. I went down the cinder track with a rubber hedge on either side, past Donald Johnson's house, past the nurses' home and over the bridge where John had been showing off on his bike and fallen head first onto the concrete below. I made my way slowly up the sandy drive to the big house and parked the car next to the ugly dome which still rose over the now empty fish pond. The garden had been swamped by the surrounding bush, the tennis court was overgrown and the fish ponds were full of rubble. The shelter had no roof and its pillars stood amidst waist high grass. There was a family living in the house and they invited us in to have a look around. As we took a final walk around the overgrown garden, it struck me how incredibly small the house seemed. After one last look from the veranda towards 23rd Avenue, I got back in my car and drove back to the hotel.

The next morning, I still hadn't decided what I was going to do with my father's ashes. I ordered a packed lunch from the hotel and drove out to the Matobo Hills. The route was so familiar that it felt as if I had never been away. The landscape had not lost any of its power.

The roads were bone dry and the ruts in them made the car, and us inside it, rattle along. Huge granite outcrops crept upon me and my sleeping child. They were gigantic presences streaked by centuries of weather. Torrential rains, and lightning, and frost had left black cracks and trails where transitory rivers had run like hair down their curved backs. The car trailed clouds of orange dust behind it, and a bright blue African sky stretched above us. I drove past dams, glittering like strips of silver in the bush. I noticed families having picnics, and others sitting on granite outcrops which stretched into the water like enormous hands. I saw herds of zebra flicking their tails, wildebeest drinking at the water's edge and the outline of a baboon here and there on the rocks. When a giraffe lumbered across the road I stopped the car and woke Delia so that she could watch it as it went on its graceful way.

I parked the car at World's View and Delia scampered off ahead of me, with her little rainbow coloured umbrella above her head. By now the heat of the midday sun was white hot and relentless. There was no shade along our path but Delia's stout little legs pumped with easy energy as she ran up the sloping path along the tops of granite boulders to the graves. The sun lit up a great dome of granite ahead of us as we made our way upwards. Delia's running about startled rainbow coloured lizards out of their sleep. They scattered in all directions, sending small showers of stones tinkering down the sloping ground. I heard the 'quare, quare' of a lowrie bird and the 'pee-o pee-o pee-o' of a hornbill.

At the top Delia skipped around looking for lizards. She used her rolled up umbrella to poke them as they lazed around in the shadows. The granite boulders looked like freakish ice cream scoops and the smaller ones like fossilised eggs put there at the beginning of time. Below us valleys carpeted with scrubland and trees arranged themselves like felt cut outs amongst the rocky outcrops. The tops of evergreen trees and swathes of bleached bush-land lay far below us and shimmered in the heat. A hot wind offered us little relief. The air vibrated off the surface of the rocks and made the sky swim in shivering waves as if in time to the trilling of the cicadas.

The sight of those magnificent boulders balancing so precariously on top of each other filled me with awe and stirred memories of all the times I had been there with my mother. Delia and I walked over to Rhodes grave. It looked like a cement wedding cake, its rectangular layers made out of chiselled slabs. An iron cover, with an inscription to the great man, radiated in the heat. The eerie wail of cicadas beating their invisible legs filled the silence in a shrill chorus. Delia stopped next to Rhodes' grave and asked me to read the inscription on the top. I started to read "here lies Cecil John Rhodes" when she interrupted me by tugging on my arm. "It's a bad, bad thing to lie, isn't it Mumma?" she said. I burst out laughing and couldn't stop, and Delia began to giggle too. Our laughter echoed out over the hills.

***

On the drive back from World's View I mulled over what to do with my father's ashes. Time was running out because I was flying back to England in two days' time. After a good night's sleep, I decided that I would scatter Norman's ashes at a local beauty spot. I drove into town and bought two red roses from a flower seller outside the City Hall. Delia sat next to me holding the roses on her lap as we drove to the Hillside Dams. The black box containing my father's ashes sat on the back seat.

There was not a soul in sight when we got to the car park. It was a warm autumnal morning and the water lilies on the dam looked faded and sad. Delia skipped over to a rocky outcrop at the far end of the lower dam. I gave her the plastic bag with the ashes in it. She danced around on the rocks, scattering her grandfather's ashes into the water. Then we walked down to the grassy area alongside the dam and we each threw a red rose as far as we could into the water. I felt nothing but relief; there were no tears. I drove to Eskimo Hut and bought us each a double scoop of vanilla ice cream in a tub smothered in a lake of shiny chocolate sauce. The following day we flew back to England and I had a strong feeling that an epic mission had been accomplished.

Not long after our return, I developed a raging fever. I went to see my doctor and explained that I had recently returned from Zimbabwe. I had a horrible feeling that I'd contracted malaria. I'd been bitten a few times during my time with John when we'd sat outside with our sundowners as dusk fell, the optimum time to be bitten by malaria-carrying mosquitoes. I had been in an emotional turmoil before I left for Zimbabwe and I'd stupidly not taken any anti-malarial prophylactics for the trip. My doctor listened politely and wondered whether it was a return of the depression which had plagued me after Delia's birth. He wrote out a prescription for an anti-depressant but agreed to take a blood sample for my own peace of mind.

The test proved positive and I spent a week in hospital. I was put on such heavy doses of quinine that the tinnitus in my ears made me temporarily deaf. Carol and Alexia looked after Delia while I was laid up. I made a speedy recovery once the treatment came to an end and have, fortunately, never had a recurrence. At the time, I was more worried about Delia because I feared that she might have contracted malaria too. Thankfully the blood tests for her were negative.

***

John got in touch to say that he and his wife had driven down to Bulawayo. They went to the Hillside Dams to say goodbye to Norman. As they were gazing into the dam near the spot where Delia had scattered Norman's ashes, an enormous water snake surfaced and gave them a fright. Just as mysteriously as it had appeared, it turned and glided away from them, back into the murk of the dam.

A year after my visit to Zimbabwe, my son David was born. Like Delia, David was born at home, in the company of Hamish and a community midwife. The joy of being able to give birth in the comfort of my familiar surroundings was matched by my terror of being inside a hospital.

PART THREE

No one is born hating another person because of the colour of his skin, or his background, or his religion.
Nelson Mandela

The grief-stricken are described as 'depressed', as if sorrow were a pathology. Mourning is work. It is not simply being sad. It is naming your pain.
Hilary Mantel

My visit to Zimbabwe in 1996
Top: The administration block where my father had his office
Right: The front door to the superintendent's house
Bottom: Sign at the entrance on 23rd Avenue
Middle: The little house
Left: My daughter standing on Rhodes' Grave in the Matobo Hills

1

My opponent is a man all dressed in white. He has a white handlebar moustache and he could be my husband, my father and Colonel Perkins mixed together. He is a formidable opponent and has every trick in the book at his disposal. He is cocky, athletic, casual, talented and very, very determined to win. He makes all the running. I can barely return his serves and his speed around the court is breathtaking.

The sun beats down on us and the man's white clothes are blindingly white. I look down and see that my takkies and my socks are stained with red dust and sweat. I am so hot that the blood is pounding inside my head and my racquet slips inside my sweaty grip. I look at it and smell it. I smell animal power. I see the same power in the yellow strings on my racquet. They are made of cat gut and every time I hit the ball I hear the sweetest sound. The wooden shaft of my racquet gleams in the sun. A smell of varnish and sweat and leather fills my head. I am playing out of my mind. I match my opponent stroke for stroke, angle for angle, power for power. White dust flies where I hit the powder dry lines on the court. I leave skid marks everywhere on its red surface.

"Advantage Cait", the umpire calls. It's match point and my serve. I put my gold St. Christopher in my mouth and beg for release. It tastes of metal and salt and it's warm against my skin. I bounce the ball lots and lots of times like I have seen Ile Nastase doing at Wimbledon. I am aiming my serve at the man's backhand. It goes exactly where I want it to go. He just gets it back with a grunt. The rally goes on and on and on. My knees are beginning to shake. I can't keep this up for much longer. I hit the ball with all the power I can find. It is an almighty forehand. The man chases madly after it and manages to hit it back between his legs. The ball sails high up into the sun. I have to shade my eyes as I stand and watch its trajectory. It seems to float in the shimmering air. "Go out, for God's sake," I mutter under my breath. "Please God, for fuck's sake, let it be out." The ball bounces just over the base line. I look at the umpire. He looks just like Maxim. He looks like an African Popeye the Sailor man with a pipe clamped between his teeth. He takes the pipe out of his mouth, stabs the air with it and yells "Out – game, set, match …."

The words are barely out of his mouth when I see my opponent rush towards the net, gesticulating wildly. "No, no, no," he is roaring. He points his racquet at the base line in disbelief. His language is fearful, obscene. He is spitting with fury. The African umpire stands his ground. "The ball was out sir. The young lady is the winner." With that my opponent rushes like a madman towards the net. He smashes his racquet against the net post over and over and over again until there is nothing left of it at all.

I go into the clubhouse to find my mother. It feels like I am walking over water. I can't wait to tell her that I have won. There she is, sitting at a table, smoking a cigarette and chatting to some of the other mothers. The smoke and her hair are the same colour. She looks up. "You look hot," she says in a matter of fact way and turns back to her friend. "I won," I say "I beat him at last. He smashed his racquet into smithereens." "Do you need a drink," my mother asks, looking inside her handbag. "Here you are darling," she says handing me some coins. "Well done love," says her friend. My mother blows a smoke ring and I can't see her clearly because of all the smoke.

I go and get a coke at the bar and wander outside with it. All I can hear is my takkies squeaking as I walk across the shining linoleum floor. I feel exhausted and exhilarated all mixed up together. The hair around my face has turned to straw and my legs ache. I need to sit down. I find some shade underneath a jacaranda tree. I make a few flowers pop by stamping on them with my takkies before I sit down on the cool earth beneath the tree.

Lying underneath it is an African woman. She is fast asleep. She wears a white doek on her head and her white apron falls away from her sleeping form. She has huge breasts and buttocks. I look at the white washed takkies she wears. They are not like mine. They are full of holes and her toes poke out of the ends.

I sit and watch as lavender blue jacaranda flowers fall like rain or confetti on top of her. Her fallen form becomes a burial mound in blue. I see all the servants who looked after me when I was young. Their white teeth fade into the clouds and the jacaranda purple turns into the azure blue of the sky.

I hear clapping in the clubhouse and wander back inside. A man with white hair is making a speech and dishing out trophies. He calls my name and helps me put on a black blazer with white lettering on the pocket. The letters flash on and off and I hear my father's chuckle. "Good old Champie". I see his bright red face grinning at me. "Good old Smithy" he says and my mother pours him another whisky. "Good old enigmatic". He smiles at me with his plastic teeth.

Suddenly his voice takes on a cold edge and I start to shake. "Things are bad" he sighs. "No news is good news". He looks at me and I look at him. "You've got to be sensibly selfish you know chum". He reaches into his pocket and takes out a syringe. Now I'm starting to sweat. I notice that his stethoscope has turned into a pair of electrodes and I think about running away. "One should never speak ill of the dead" my father says with real menace. He starts towards me and I know he's going to smack me. I jerk sideways. He breathes heavily through his nose and he starts to hit me. "Honour thy father and thy mother that thy days may be long upon the land" he says in time to beating me. "Keep quiet or you'll wake up the whole bladdy place" he shouts and slams my door shut.

I wake up with a jolt. My heart is pounding, my breath is shallow and I'm shaking from head to foot. My sheets are damp with sweat.

2

In 1992, when I went to Toronto to visit my mother in the hospital, my father came to have supper at Monique's apartment one evening. I remember picking up a soap-stone carving of an African man's head and asking him about it. He replied that my mother had given it to him as an anniversary present. My father said: "A bloke once picked up that thing. Yurra, man, I thought he was going to hit me on the head with it. Bladdy scary I can tell you chum." I held that heavy head in both hands, and thought that it was true - it would smash someone's skull to a pulp. "Ja, bladdy poofta that bloke was too" my father said. "Thought he could get me to sign him off from being called up. The bloke went berserk when he realised he wasn't going to pull the wool over my eyes." My father shook his head, laughed his snorty laugh and took another sip of his whisky.

***

Many years later John got in touch to ask if I knew someone called Roseanna Waters. He said someone by that name had posted a message on his Facebook page, hoping to make contact with me. I didn't recognise her surname but I immediately knew that it was Roseanna Baxter. Roseanna and I exchanged many emails and, eventually, I asked her what she knew about her father's death.

Roseanna wrote:

> *"We lived in Ingutsheni for two years during the early 60's while my father completed his psychiatric degree. During his finals, my mother took us kids to Cape Town to visit family. My father was supposed to join us after a week but tragically died during a home experiment with LSD, a very new and exciting drug at the time. He should have had another doctor with him during the experiment but it seemed this person never arrived and he continued to do the experiment on himself alone. On my mother's return the head nun, Mother Alana told her about the experiment and said that it was such a pity that my father had not waited for the other doctor to be present. This is how we knew what had happened. Unfortunately during my father's years as a medical student he was always willing to be the guinea pig and have the other students practice on him, so his behaviour was true to his character.*

This tragic event ended my magical time as a child roaming the huge grounds of Ingutsheni. I always yearned to see you again. We never got a chance to say goodbye and to keep in touch. Thank goodness for Facebook!"

Roseanna told me that Dr. Montgomery eventually testified that he and Roger had planned an experiment. The coroner ruled that Roger's death was "death by misadventure" and so Trudy was able to give him a Catholic burial.

When I told a friend about how Roseanna had found me on Facebook and recounted how her father had been found dead next door, she looked at me and said "It sounds like that doctor might have been murdered. Have you ever considered that?" I didn't tell her that I had indeed considered it; that I had imagined my father sneaking next door and murdering Roger Baxter for having an affair with my mother. I'd also imagined that one of the nurses had been caught stealing drugs by Roger, and he or she had crept over from the nurses' home and suffocated him in his bed, before putting him in the bath with a plastic bag over his head.

I continued to ask Roseanna questions about her father's death. She told me that Roger was in the process of applying for a job abroad and had just given her a new bicycle for Christmas when he died. A year later, I emailed Roseanna a copy of the letter my mother had written about the day her father was found. Roseanna said that none of them knew about the plastic bag over her father's head. I felt concerned that I'd spoiled her fantasy that her father's death was accidental. I came to accept that it was likely that Roger was struggling. It is probable, given the conditions and the degree of suffering inside Ingutsheni, that at the start of a New Year, he had decided that he could not carry on with his chosen profession.

***

Roseanna's news about her father's experiments with drugs opened a door into a world I hadn't considered in much depth. Memories began to surface and I thought back to something that happened when I was about ten years old. I'd been hitting a tennis ball against the servants' quarters in the boiling sun and went to get a drink out of the fridge.

My mother wrote:

> *"I remember you drinking something, am not sure it was benzene though – why would it have been in the fridge? You took a bottle from the fridge thinking it was water and drank a sip – Lesley grabbed the bottle from you."*

I spat whatever was in the bottle in the sink. Lesley snatched it out of my hands and read the label. I remember the worried look on my mother's face when she asked me how much of it I'd drunk and there was some talk about me having to go to hospital. It tasted so foul that I knew I hadn't swallowed any of it. Later, over dinner, my father laughed and told my mother to make sure that the servants stopped putting benzene in the fridge. It dawned on me that the label that Lesley read on the bottle was not 'benzene' but "Benzodiazepine", the generic name for the tranquilisers that were the new wonder drugs at the time. This revelation made me realise that Roger Baxter and Dr. Montgomery were not the only doctors at Ingutsheni who were dabbling in drugs. It's likely that my father had begun to self-medicate in order to cope with his work.

John remembered another incident when we started going to tennis parties. He wrote:

> *"I remember the time Elspeth forgot to fetch us from a party at the Bulawayo Sports Club. You and I waited til well after midnight and then decided to walk back to Ingutsheni. It must have taken us about two hours."*

My mother was probably taking Valium to help her cope too.

***

I thought back to my experience of having the measles in 1966. It coincided with Trudy Baxter's return to Bulawayo for the inquest into her husband's death. During her visit, she gave my mother a gift for me from Roseanna - the Pocketful of Proverbs - and it had upset me that Roseanna wasn't next door any more. I believe my father diagnosed my distress as hysteria and gave me a dose of Largactil. I hallucinated and saw little green men on my pillow. My father said that I had the measles, but I was only ill for one night. My mother tended to me believing that I was running a fever. I don't remember having a rash.

My parents didn't attend Roger's funeral; I imagine that it took place in South Africa.

***

I began to mull over other diagnoses that my father had made. I asked Monique about the time she had her appendix out.

She wrote:

> "I had my appendix out when I worked at the bakery so I suppose I must have been around eighteen. The only other thing I remember was having pneumonia at the little house and having hallucinations of little men like gnomes climbing up my mosquito net, apparently from the high temperature I think but as for measles or chicken pox, don't think so. I did have whooping cough when we lived in England. If I remember more in the middle of the night will let you know."

I wondered if Monique's memories of pneumonia together with the hallucinations she recalled were linked to the time that John was diagnosed with pneumonia at ten months old. I believe that, in fact, my father gave Monique a dose of Largactil when she'd expressed anxiety or unhappiness about having another new baby in the house. With some alarm, I thought back to my mother's description of John's sudden admission to hospital. I believe that my father gave us two younger children a sedative because we were waking up so regularly at Ingutsheni. I believe he gave me and John the same dose, and my little brother could not be roused. I realised, to my horror, that my father had very likely sedated us at night for a sustained period of time and that's why I've had such terrible nightmares. My recurring one about being swept over the Devil's Cataract finally made sense. All my life I had woken up suddenly, like surfacing out of no man's land. I realised that I'd probably seldom, if ever, experienced a normal night's sleep since I was an infant.

***

Alarm bells started to ring about experiments with drugs, and I wondered how Mother Alana knew about them. My mother once

157

said that it was only right and proper that doctors used the inmates at Ingutsheni as guinea pigs. It gave them a purpose in life, she said. It was good for them to be making a contribution towards medical science and to society in general. I thought about the silent children I'd seen at the St. Francis Home and I wondered what else Mother Alana knew about drugs. I wondered what happened to the children's bodies when they died.

***

I began to think more deeply about the inmates who worked in our garden and the escapees that Roseanna and I saw at the quarry. I began to suffer from awful nightmares in which I was constantly running away - I ran over burning bridges, along blind alleys, fell off cliffs into torrents of bubbling lava and struggled to keep myself safe under avalanches that cascaded on top of me. During this un-nerving process, various other pennies began to drop.

I was fourteen when my father diagnosed me with appendicitis. I remember telling him that I was worried about a school test, that I was anxious about revising without my mother's help because she and Monique were away visiting Lesley. I have no memory of being in pain; just suffering from 'butterflies' at having to sit a test. I asked John what he remembered about the time my mother and Monique went to visit Lesley.

He wrote:

"When Elspeth and Monique went to England to visit Lesley, Norman put us both in the Mater Dei! He felt we would be better looked after there than at home. 1969 was a dreadful year for us both – I also had my appendix removed that year and I had jaundice. I was in Standard Five. I was very sick with jaundice in 1969 – I think I caught it from picking my nose and eating what I found! Elspeth and Norman moved me into their bedroom for a time, I didn't go to hospital for the jaundice but I was off school for six weeks possibly longer. I remember trying to walk to the bathroom and falling over. I was delirious for some time and had the most terrible headaches. Not long after I had recovered from jaundice I started getting stomach pains. Elspeth took me to the doctor. He stuck his massive hand into

158

my stomach. It hurt like mad, so he said he had better take my appendix out. I was in the Mater Dei for a week or ten days.

Dr Nixon could see the whites of my eyes had started to turn yellow and suspected jaundice when he came to see me. Elspeth was upset because she had shouted at me and told me to stop being silly. She thought I was play acting because I hated my teacher and didn't want to go to school because I couldn't do my homework. She'd tried to help me do it the night before."

Monique's experience of having her appendix out had resulted in her being in hospital for a while, so she had unwittingly set a precedent for myself and John. I was shocked at John's open assertion that he and I were hospitalised so that the nuns would take care of us while our mother was away. John's recollection of our admission to the Mater Dei Hospital was a clear acknowledgement that my father had used his influence to get us admitted. I hadn't realised he'd been admitted to the Mater Dei at the same time as me. I wonder what 'illness' my father had dreamed up? It's probable that he gave John Largactil before and during his hospitalisation, and that he continued to do so while I recovered from my surgery. John's memories of having yellow jaundice and then having his appendix removed were classic side effects associated with Largactil. John has been found to have liver damage which is also associated with prolonged use of Largactil. He never was addicted to exercise like me and his weight gain in later life has put him at risk of developing diabetes.

***

I've mulled over my father's comments about my being in a "dwaal"; it's an Afrikaans word which means 'a sort of stupor'. I considered the 'benzene' scenario in more detail. I suspect he added a few drops of a tranquiliser to a health tonic my mother gave me to keep my strength up around exam time. It was an orange flavoured tonic called Vi-Daylin. When I remember how often I used to sip a spoon of it as a pick-me-up, and how lethargic I felt during the long years that I lived at Ingutsheni, I suspect this is what he did. Perhaps he believed it would help to calm my nerves. These realisations loomed out of a fog. The new wonder drugs and tranquilisers like Valium were hailed in the 1960's and 1970's as cures for all sorts of mental health conditions, especially in treating depression, anxiety and insomnia. What my father did was not that surprising when I considered the freedom he had as a psychiatrist at Ingutsheni. There were no inspections and he was accountable to no one as a senior member of staff.

***

One evening I met up with an old school friend who had been on the geography expedition with me to Mushandike in 1972. I reminded her about my drunk and disorderly behaviour and how I'd made such a spectacle of myself that the headmistress had threatened to expel me. She stared at me in blank surprise. I was insistent: "Don't you remember how I'd lain on the ground and sang a silly song about The Lord's Prayer?" She shook her head and said that there had been nothing wrong with my behaviour at all. She remembered that we had all fallen for the game rangers, and we reminisced about which one we'd fancied the most. As I drove home that evening, I felt outraged. I remembered how ashamed I'd felt in the weeks after the Mushandike trip, and how I couldn't face going to school. I thought back to how my father said I was suffering from alcohol poisoning. My mother sent me for blood and urine tests which my father insisted were abnormal. Every evening when he came home, he stood at my door and asked: "So, how's sicky today?" I spent three months in bed and missed my Matric exams, which would have guaranteed me a place at a South African university. It put extra pressure on me the following year, when I had to pass my A Levels, or I would not have been able to go to university.

***

During our reminiscing about our childhood, I discovered that Norman used to invite Lesley or Monique or John to his office, where he would get a tray of refreshments and biscuits delivered for afternoon tea. They each remember being taken into the hospital dining room and being shown around the wards. I was never included. I didn't have piano or ballet lessons like my sisters. I wasn't taken to watch cricket or rugby matches by my father like John was. John went fishing, water-skiing and flying with his friend Aaron, whose father was one of Norman's medical colleagues. I didn't travel abroad with my mother. I was left to my own devices.

160

My father said to each of us at different times in our lives: "*You are unrealistic, self-deceptive, deluded, selfish, childish and immature*". He said this often and with such conviction that I believed him. John called him 'the boss'. I remember Monique saying that Norman was 'like a bad penny that just kept coming back'. I called him 'the doom and gloom man'. I used to pray that he'd die so that our mother would take us to live in England and be reunited with Lesley. My mother used to say how nice it would be if, one day, we could all live there.

I look back in awe at my solitary existence at Ingutsheni. I see that winning at tennis and performing to a high standard at school provided me with a tantalising fantasy that I might be loved and accepted by everyone. Such short-lived moments of triumph could never compensate me for my loneliness. I remember after Delia was born, and I was diagnosed with post-natal depression, I told my health visitor that I had a problem with reality. My baby's arrival, and especially her cries and screams, awoke deep inside me the terrors of my early childhood that I couldn't put into words.

3

Unlike the Victorian asylums on which Ingutsheni was modelled, there was no chapel on the grounds and no final resting place for any of the dead. I don't know how many people died inside Ingutsheni's overcrowded and noisy wards during the time that we lived there. I believe that the bodies of white patients like Jamie's mother were quietly cremated and the family notified by the hospital authorities. I have since learned that African patients whose bodies were unclaimed would have been buried in unmarked graves by prisoners requisitioned from Khami Maximum prison to carry out the burials. The nuns at St. Francis made arrangements for the bodies of children who died in their care.

My parents told me that 'Ingutsheni' meant 'place of blankets'. I learned that at one time in Ingutsheni's history there were over eight hundred patients crammed into wards designed to hold a quarter of that number. They only had four toilets at their disposal. I discovered that the name 'Ingutsheni' was taken from the isiNdebele language and corrupted by the British colonial authorities. I learned that the asylum was built on or close to one of three royal settlements which belonged to the Ndebele King Lobengula. The settlement where Ingutsheni Lunatic Asylum was built in 1908 was called 'Engutsheni'. The fort which Donald Johnson drew on his map of Ingutsheni was a relic from the king's settlement at Engutsheni.

I also learned that an 'Ingubo' was a regiment of the King's protective warriors, a bit like the regulars in the territorial army who assist citizens with civic duties, and who are usually called upon in times of need. These warriors wore a particular kind of tribal blanket. When white doctors asked African patients questions like "Where are you?" and "Why have you been sent here?" - they were expecting the inmates to reply that they were at a mental hospital for people suffering from madness (in isiNdebele the word 'inhlanya' means 'mad people' and 'enhlanyeni' means 'place of mad people'). Many replied that they were at the place of King Lobengula's wives. Their words were taken by the psychiatrists at Ingutsheni as proof that they had lost touch with reality and were, indeed, insane.

I discovered that Africans were given higher voltage electrical shocks during ECT treatment than white patients, and they were not given adequate anaesthesia. An inmate at Ingutsheni might receive hundreds of rounds of ECT during his or her time as a patient there. Every Saturday morning my father went to the Nervous Disorders Hospital to administer Electric Convulsant Therapy (ECT) on his European patients. When ECT failed to pacify certain patients an operation called a leucotomy was performed. It involved the use of an ice-pick-like-instrument (a steel leucome) to sever the frontal lobe and thalamus regions of the brain.

Many African patients were suffering from malnutrition and other preventable diseases. They earned a pittance working as farm labourers, miners and domestic servants - and food shortages became rife during droughts which were severely exacerbated as the Rhodesian war progressed. Ntete, like many of the inmates at Ingutsheni, suffered from the advanced stages of venereal disease. His face was covered in pimples. Venereal disease was rampant in the male ghettos created by the mining industry in Rhodesia where workers were given inadequate housing in segregated compounds, cut off from their wives and families. The colonial authorities referred to this and other diseases like pellagra (associated with poor nutrition) as 'diseases of employment'.

Unlike the European patients who slept on beds, the African inmates at Ingutsheni were made to sleep on concrete floors with only a thin blanket to keep them warm during the winter months, when temperatures at night could fall below freezing. Heavy doses of medication and the effect of shock treatment and leucotomies prevented them from being able to regulate their body temperature normally. It's likely that many of the inmates at Ingutsheni succumbed to death from hypothermia and medical neglect. I imagine Ntete died of general paralysis of the insane or syphilis of the brain, a serious neurological disorder as a result of syphilis being left untreated.

***

It's terrible that people suffering from epilepsy were admitted to a place like Ingutsheni. Epilepsy is not a mental illness. It is a non-communicable metabolic disability. In England, people who suffer

163

from epilepsy have been helped with appropriate medication, to the extent that people with mild forms of epilepsy lead normal lives. Furthermore, specially trained dogs can sense abnormal electrical activity in the brain, and thus alert their owners about an imminent seizure. A sufferer can then go and lie down somewhere safe until the seizure has passed.

The notion that an epileptic has been cursed by a wicked spirit is still widely believed in Zimbabwe. Touching foaming saliva or stepping in urine (during a seizure the bladder is released) is considered dangerous because 'ngozi' (an evil spirit) is said to be associated with these excretions. The stigma is particularly onerous for women who fear that no one will want to marry them. In Zimbabwe, where the health care infrastructure has collapsed there is only one MRI scanner in the country. Medication is in desperately short supply and so epileptics get injured during seizures, the most common injury being the result of serious burns from falling into fires used for cooking. Epileptics in Zimbabwe suffer financial hardships through being injured, due to subsequent loss of earnings and having to pay for treatment. Epilepsy is also linked to autism and so it's likely that many of Ingutsheni's inmates would today be on the autistic spectrum. Many of the sounds I heard through the hibiscus hedge resembled those made by non-verbal people on the severest end of the autistic spectrum. The fact that drugs and shock treatment were administered to such vulnerable members of society has been an appalling discovery to make.

It's also sad to think that poliomyelitis victims were admitted to a place like Ingutsheni. I believe that the way that society cares for its most vulnerable people is a hidden world because we're all frightened by the fact that any form of incapacity could happen to us too. The people left alone to care for the most vulnerable are burdened with society's collective fear and ignorance.

4

The liberation struggle in Zimbabwe began in 1896. I learned that the maxim gun enabled white settlers to defeat the first native insurrection against the British South Africa Company's administration. I thought back to Colonel Perkins and his African helpers, Willard and Maxim. I thought back to the electric machine that Maxim man-handled in order to fire balls over the net and I felt a deep sense of outrage. Willard is a name associated with a woman who campaigned for emancipation and education; it was also the name of a brand of crisps that were a popular snack in Rhodesia. I felt ashamed of myself for my ignorance and my respect for Colonel Perkins' disintegrated.

When I went back to Zimbabwe in 1996, I took Delia to look around my old senior school. We called in at the headmistress's office to ask her permission to walk around the grounds of the school. An African man knocked on her door while we were talking and immediately recognised me. It was Willard. I discovered that he had become the tennis coach at my old secondary school.

***

During the colonial era, African women were not given an identification document (known as a 'situpa' which allowed African men to live and work in European areas). African women were considered by the white population as too backward to educate into Western domestic duties. They were at a double disadvantage if they didn't learn to speak 'fanakalo' because this meant that even domestic servant jobs were hard to come by. As a result an African woman who was picked up by the police or handed over by her family to the authorities was in a precarious position. Many found their way into Ingutsheni simply for being unable to explain themselves in an intelligible way. During the sixteen years that I lived there, I never saw an African female inmate out and about within the grounds of Ingutsheni.

***

I learned that the rain dance which my mother performed during a drought when white people were praying for rain has no relation to prayer, but is rather a choreographed re-enactment of the experience of rain falling. When African women perform a rain dance, their clapping hands echo the thunder claps heralding the rain, their drumming feet mimic the rain drumming on the parched earth, and their ululating voices express the relief and joy that rain brings to people with the promise of renewed life.

When I went to a Ladysmith Black Mambazo concert during the writing of this book, I was shocked by the realisation that I'd seen some of the inmates who worked in our garden performing fragments of traditional dances and songs – that these were broken memories and not symptoms of their 'madness'.

***

In certain academic circles, it is generally known that the Smith regime used biological weapons on rural populations during the Rhodesian war. Anthrax spores were introduced to wells and rivers so that people and animals contracted anthrax and died. Under the Smith regime the brutal suppression of political activists was regarded as a white prerogative. However the contamination of rivers and wells, as well as the poisoning of clothing worn by people believed to be sympathetic towards freedom fighters was something I knew nothing about and this shocked me deeply. Maximum security prisons like Chikurubi and Khami were holding facilities and places of torture during the Rhodesian war. I read about detention centres called Gonakudzingwa, Sikombela and Wha Wha that I'd not heard of before. For the African inmates at Ingutsheni, the conditions inside the hospital bore an uncanny resemblance to those detention centres, with the additional horror of mind-altering drugs, shock treatment, lobotomies and leucotomies - all of which were treatments my father carried out on people placed under his care. I discovered that there were other medical personnel who regarded the Africans in their care with callous indifference.

***

African culture has an impressive oral and musical tradition. Africa is a continent which is regarded as the cradle of humanity. I discovered that the Matobo Hills, where Cecil John Rhodes and other white heroes are buried, is a place of great spiritual significance for the indigenous people of Zimbabwe. In terms of importance it is equivalent to the sanctity that Westminster Abbey holds for the people of Great Britain.

The nomadic herders who once populated the Matobo Hills were dispossessed of their cattle, their way of life and their land, and the Matopos became a recreational national park for the enjoyment of local Europeans and travellers from around the world. My mother used to take me and John for picnics in the Matopos. She took us to the Maleme Dams where she had to navigate the Citroen over a narrow causeway to get to the campsite. I remember how we used to scramble our way to the top of a kopje of granite boulders where we sat and looked out over the dam. We spent hours watching fish eagles swoop out over the water hoping for a catch. We would watch the wind sweep patterns on the surface of the dam and shout our names so that our voices echoed back to us from over the hills.

***

I remember how we used to visit the Bambata Caves during our picnics and how I traced my fingers over ancient rock paintings of human figures and wild animals. I learned that many of the caves in the Matobo Hills are still regarded as sacred shrines where spiritualists go in order to consult with ancestors and to perform rituals concerned with water and fertility. Such rituals were performed at life-giving rock pools, streams and rivers, and also to herald the coming of the rains.

***

I learned that Rhodes was greatly impressed by the discovery of King Mzilikazi's tomb in a cave at Entumbane in the eastern area of the Matobo Hills. Mzilikazi was King before Lobengula – it was he who founded the Matabele Kingdom. His body, placed in a stone chair, was found in an upright position surveying the beautiful expanse of land that he had conquered. This discovery inspired Cecil John Rhodes to choose the Matobo Hills as his final resting place. He saw himself as Mzilikazi's spiritual equal, and the supreme ruler over the British territory named after him. Rhodes even went so far as to have Mzilikazi's skull measured in order to gauge the Ndebele king's brain capacity.

167

***

Today the Matopos National Park is a world heritage site and Rhodes Grave is still a pilgrimage for visitors from all over the world.

Sadly, Ingutsheni, *place of blankets*, offered shelter from the elements but not from man's inhumanity to man. Post-Independence, Ingutsheni gradually succumbed to financial neglect by the ruling party. Conditions inside the hospital have remained extremely difficult.

5

In the developed world people are living longer and many have the luxury of trawling through genealogy sites and other records on the internet, researching their family histories. The last thing in the world I wanted to do was explore my family history. I knew it would cause me a great deal of pain. I looked into the darkest shadows of my past and was appalled at what I found. I saw how white people had manipulated and segregated a whole nation in order to exploit its mineral wealth, its natural beauty and its hard-working people. Many of us amassed staggering amounts of wealth and most of us lived a luxurious life-style equivalent to the upper classes in Great Britain, being waited on hand and foot by dark-skinned servants who not only cooked and cleaned but also looked after the very old and the very young; mothers like mine had the freedom to lead carefree lives. I enjoyed top class schooling, health care, housing and hospitality at the expense of the indigenous people around me who had to struggle and fight for equal access to the institutions they helped to build for us – with no vote, no right of abode, little financial reward, no sick pay, no pension rights and no concern for their health and safety. Exploitation and indifference lay at the heart of my childhood. Hatred was aimed at Africans and other races. Anyone stupid was usually the subject of Rhodesian jokes – which invariably included people with learning difficulties and especially Africans.

After the stormy night when my mother took John into her arms, I found myself at my father's mercy. There was no evidence my father felt kindness or concern for those of us he considered of lesser worth. Whatever awareness my father had of the power of the mind, he had little regard for the power of other peoples' minds. He viewed all artistic expression as a symptom of insanity, all forms of happiness as a sign of hubris and all financial gain as proof of moral rectitude.

As an adult, I made works of art in an effort to express myself. I wrote poetry because I needed to put my outrage into words. To my amazement, when I started talking about writing a memoir, I was met with a lot of interest. People lent me books and gave me recommendations for further reading. I was invited to join the

Britain-Zimbabwe Society. There I met colonials like myself, writers, academics, anthropologists, social workers, teachers, psychiatrists and therapists. I talked to African members of BZS who came to give papers in the UK. I met many committed and courageous people from Zimbabwe. I listened to their stories and shared in their enthusiasm for their people and their country despite the hardships, the corruption and the intimidation by members of the ruling party. Many of these people commended me for my determination to tell my story and so gave me the courage to keep writing.

Ingutsheni was built by colonial authorities who, together with the psychiatrists they employed, indiscriminately defined vast numbers of people as 'trouble' rather than human beings in distress. Psychiatric language is tremendously frightening. Its medical approach is a quagmire of diagnoses, drugs and dogma. I wrote because I had to make sense of something that terrified me. Words loomed out of the fog of my remembering and filled me with anxiety: rejected, ostracised, shunned, excommunicated, disowned, cut off, unwanted, abandoned, left out, dispossessed, ignored, forgotten, condemned, written off, silenced – banished. My father used words associated with schizophrenia to define me when I was unhappy or he thought I'd stepped out of line. He interpreted my feelings as symptoms of ill health and moral failure. I suffered agonies trying to figure out what was wrong with me. As I researched the past, I began to fear desperately for his patients as well as for myself. I feared for his African patients - particularly the African women I never saw but whose voices I heard crying out.

In the end I had to write to keep my terror from consuming me. I needed to make my presence felt, to stand up for myself, to see where I was. My thoughts about myself invariably took me back to Ingutsheni. I realised that it wasn't the abandoned children, the nuns with their fixed smiles, or even the screaming patients that frightened me out of my wits. It was my father's certainty and his obvious contentment with his diagnoses. His physical violence was easy to remember. It was his scorn and his smugness that lay at the heart of my terror. I laughed at myself in the same derisory fashion as my father did. I saw that my thoughts and feelings were of little consequence; that I too had dismissed them as utterly ridiculous. I saw that I'd gone about my life believing that the views of others outweighed my meagre offerings - offerings made more meagre by my inability to express myself. I carried my father's way of relating with me into all my relationships. I expected people to laugh at me and speak to me as if I were a lunatic. The more they did, the more at home I felt. I had no words for my feelings. My heart sinks, remembering that I could never feel sad, angry, joyful, mischievous or afraid without feeling like a criminal. In my troubling dreams I didn't see myself as a girl; I was always a boy, sometimes a curly-haired dog, swept up in an atmosphere of impending disaster.

This turmoil lay buried for the best part of my life. So profoundly was I affected by the isolation of my childhood that I couldn't tell the difference between excitement and fear; there were many words like sad, angry, anxious, frustrated and jealous were not part of my vocabulary. Such emotional illiteracy might be called 'evil' or 'mad'; I guess my father would have called such a state of affairs 'pathological'. I was incapable of differentiating hatred from love and therefore from knowing the guiding force of my life. I was as ignorant as any bird, beast or living thing struggling to cope with an alienating predicament.

At Ingutsheni the sounds of people laughing, chatting or mowing the lawn were rare; I never heard the voices of children playing together. I missed vital cues in facial expression and body language by having so few friends come over to play; I didn't learn how to debate or to negotiate. I depended on our family conversations until I was in my teens. I was very timid at school. I didn't know what it meant to be an emotional human being until I sat and wrote this all down. I feel like a flood has receded from my mind and that my heart has been released from a terror of utter destitution.

In my father's world there was never any credit given to me for figuring things out as I went along through my life, nor was there anyone there for me to hold onto when I couldn't figure things out and felt lost. There was no room for doubt or for making errors. I was supposed to be happy, successful, independent and unquestioning. I was expected to perform like an automaton and when I didn't or couldn't my father said that I was suffering from an illness.

It wasn't love or playing sport that saved me from the insanity of my childhood. Lesley and Monique listened incessantly to pop music on their radios and record players in the early 1960's. The healing balm of beautiful and inspirational songs – the sound of people making music together - has always lifted my spirits and given me comfort.

When I came to live in London in 1986, I discovered books and art and began to explore African music and to read widely about African culture. I sought psychological help and started to think for myself.

Epilogue

Philosophers, theologians and writers of all persuasions are prone to make broad statements about what it means to be a human being. I've asked myself whether their pronouncements can be true, for they don't include humans whose brains are damaged, or whose brains are too immature or too old to function well enough for them to think, speak and act in their own interests. It seems to me that the truth is as variable as there are human brains to contemplate what it is to be alive on this beautiful blue planet. I am convinced, however, that when men, women and children are encouraged to identify, own and share their feelings, the world might become less dangerously volatile on the one hand, and less doggedly indifferent on the other. Emotions, after all, are our common ground and they are also our prime motivators in life.

Historically, philosophical and religious statements have been made by men. The vast majority of men remain un-involved in caring for their own children. The founders of the great innovations in psychiatric expertise have all been men. Fathers have been excluded, or have chosen to exclude themselves, from the immense emotional challenge of raising a child. The significant economic sacrifice of caring for very young children impacts mothers more than fathers. Psychological research has tended to focus on white student populations, so our knowledge about well-being is severely limited. Mothers know first-hand that diversity is the way of all flesh; there are no ideal children - just noisy, messy, fearful, mischievous, funny, adventurous, needy, curious, innocent, emotional, communicative kids. I believe there is heroism involved in being a mother – to give of one's body, mind and heart for the well-being of another person. The challenge of raising a disabled or brain-injured child can't be under-estimated and shouldn't be the sole responsibility of any woman. All too often, however, because of the isolation and financial encumbrance involved, marriages buckle and many women are left to care alone and in isolation for a child with special needs. In previous generations, such women had the additional disadvantage of having to endure the belief from some quarters that they were being punished by God, or cursed by an evil spirit, for bearing such a child.

I look back at the history of my childhood. I look back at the power bestowed on me as a white child in Africa. I see myself hitting Ntete in the face with a mud-ball and thinking nothing of it. I look back at African squads toiling in our garden, as thin as scarecrows, bare-headed, their feet baking on the hot earth; their place in the world seemed as ordinary to me as the sun that shone down and the rains that provided us with life. I will never forget them nor the terrible screams that I heard at Ingutsheni.

Life is never static. Each of us experiences a continuous ebb and flow of thoughts and feelings as we live every day of our lives. We figure things out as time unfolds and we interact with objects and each other as we develop our ideas. From the moment we are born, we rely on one another for information about how the world works. Perhaps humans are not so different from starlings whose murmurations create patterns that sweep and swirl in unison until they find a warm, safe place to congregate. Perhaps this is how best to describe an accumulation of wisdom and the way that humanity evolves. Being a loner, an outsider or going against the tide is very difficult; being cut off from any form of dialogue with another person is extremely limiting. It can make the world feel like a very scary place.

***

Each day I live my life. I climb into my car and go to work; I shop, prepare food, meet friends, sit in front of my computer, watch television, spend time with my family and get into my comfortable bed at night. I realise that millions of hands have created the world in which I live. I am no more independent or perfectible than a wave that rolls its way towards its inevitable end.

***

I've asked myself many questions about mental health during the process of writing this book. Questions like - how seriously does a psychiatrist consider domestic violence, economic deprivation, traumatic life experiences, religious beliefs, family dynamics and other significant relationships when making a mental health assessment? How much are cultural differences explored within psychiatry? How much has psychiatric practice changed since my father practised? Are prescription drugs necessary, and if so, for how long? Whose interests are best served by psychiatrists – the medical profession, society, the state, the pharmaceutical industry, the patients or the psychiatrists themselves? What exactly is a 'mental illness' and who suffers from 'it'? Does anyone really know what mental health looks like? Since we are all born inherently different, what does 'normal' brain function mean? Where does mental health begin and end? How do people cope with poverty, illness, disability, domestic violence, rape, war and death? Psychiatry is based on a medical model of human health; as far as I know, psychiatric training doesn't require personal therapy or counselling, and a psychiatrist does not have a personal supervisor with whom to meet on a regular basis for support and on-going guidance. What emotional and psychological support is given to mental health professionals in order for them, in turn, to best support distressed, often learning-disabled, and sometimes violent, clients? My father's only confidant was my mother. He had built up such an aura of expertise about himself that there was no room for him to express whatever feelings of self-doubt or fatigue he must have experienced.

The care of needy people is unrelenting, demanding and exhausting – something for which my father was fundamentally ill-equipped. Both my parents lacked an extended family who might have given them emotional and moral support. The fact that care, shelter, nutrition and medication are regarded as profitable commodities is a growing reality in the world today. An illness, an accident or having to care for a dependent can catapult a person into a major crisis and crippling poverty. Time spent with the very young, the very old and the very incapable may seem unproductive but its solace can't be measured. I believe that prescription drugs and mind-altering substances can add to human misery, may contribute to the demise of everyday compassion and facilitate the exploitation and abuse of vulnerable people. Throwing money, drugs and technology into healthcare, without also training, supporting and retaining compassionate humans to care for other humans can end up dehumanising everyone.

My father's world, with its Orthodox ideals and prohibitions - its gendered apartheid - had a simplistic moral code that divided life into opposing forces. My father belonged to a club where individualism, heroism and competition ruled the day. The fact that he was Jewish and a psychiatrist might well have contributed to him becoming a compassionate person. Tragically, his beliefs prevented him from being the vulnerable and fallible human being that he was. For me, and for many of his patients, it was our vulnerability - our fearful cries - that fuelled his need to label us and to silence us.

It's sad to see that my father simply exchanged the dogmatic belief system of his Orthodox Jewish upbringing for the dogmatic belief system of psychiatric practice. I believe that psychiatric practice has not changed enough since my father's day not just in Zimbabwe, but in psychiatric institutions throughout the world. Trauma, in all its different forms, requires compassionate education, kindness, sensitive insight and long term friendly support for a sustained recovery. The trauma of early childhood neglect is particularly difficult to put into words because a sufferer is so used to living in silence and in fear. When I've talked to people about this book, they have invariably felt free to tell me heart-breaking stories about their own experiences, or that of relatives and friends, within the psychiatric system.

There were other institutions like Ingutsheni built under colonial rule in Africa and elsewhere. I wonder just how many inmates' stories will never be told.

It's taken a life time for me to tell mine.

Acknowledgements

I'm grateful to my friends, some of whom kindly read drafts of this book and all of whom have listened to me talking about my childhood.

There are many people who've helped me give voice to my experience, to express my hunger for social justice and to come to terms with the tragedy of my childhood. I would like to commend Lynette A. Jackson for researching and writing about Ingutsheni's background and its place in the colonial history of Zimbabwe. Significant writers, philosophers and artists include Viktor Frankl, Martin Buber, Soren Kierkegaard, Doris Lessing, Dorothy Rowe, Bruce Perry and Maia Szalavitz, Jon Allen, Roy F. Baumeister, Babette Rothschild, Bessel van der Kolk, Dr. Ronald Doctor, Marshall Rosenberg, Terence Ranger, Chinua Achebe, Arandhati Roy, Kazuo Ishiguro, Nadine Gordimer, Jenny Saville, Andre Brink, Yael Farber, Noviolet Bulawayo, Miriam Makeba, Oliver Mtukudzi, Fela Kuti, Siyaya and The Missa Luba - amongst others. I'm indebted to Marieke Faber Clarke, Pathisa Nyathi, Simukai Chigudu, Patricia Battye and Paul Hubbard for sharing their knowledge of Zimbabwe's history with me. I'm grateful to Phil Cox for his work on the complex ethics of the Hippocratic Oath - to 'first, do no harm' - and the importance for professionals to be able to admit, share, discuss and learn from the mistakes and difficulties that inevitably arise in the care of vulnerable and troubled people.

I couldn't have survived living at Ingutsheni without my siblings or the friendship of the Baxters next door. Lesley and Monique have given me love, support and strength in so many different ways. We each owe Monique and Jamie a tremendous debt of gratitude for the way that they loved and cared for our parents in their old age. I'm especially grateful to John for being my companion in a place that was so removed from the commonplace and the nostalgic. John's humour and his horror of fanaticism helped keep me sane. Without doubt he bore the brunt of my fear and my aggression. The result was that both of us got into hot water with one or other of our parents as regularly as clockwork. I'm sure my mother never imagined she'd raise her children inside a lunatic asylum in Africa. She believed implicitly in Norman and his expertise; after my grandmother died she had no one else with whom to confer, and her ignorance of sibling rivalry with its fiery mixture of envy, loyalty, love and hatred remained absolute. My father's intolerance of family dynamics was no help to any of us. My mother added considerably to my love of art by hanging prints by Vincent van Gogh and Toulouse Lautrec in the dining room of the big house and by taking me on regular visits to the Jairos Jiri and Mzilikazi Craft Centres in Bulawayo. She passed on her passion for flowering plants and for animals. She did the best she knew how given the circumstances of her life and the nature of her marriage.

I am indebted to my husband Hamish and his family for their love and financial support. I am profoundly grateful to my children, Delia and David, for helping me reconnect with the child that I once was – without you I would not have found the courage to travel all the way back to my earliest memories and face them. Bringing this story to fruition has occupied me for eight years; working my way through the traumatic events of my childhood resulted in a lot of sleepless nights. I needed time to write everything down; to mourn all the love that might have been but never was.

I could not have seen this process through without having people to talk to. I owe my loving heart to Mary, Margaret, Anderson, Shadrick, Moses, Bernard and Martha – thanks for being part of my life. Being listened to with interest can't be measured or treasured enough; being on the receiving end of human warmth has been the best antidote for the loneliness and segregation of my childhood.

I owe my sanity to the psychotherapists who have listened to me with compassion and respect. Thanks especially to Lea who has read every word I've written since I started talking to her after my daughter was seriously injured in a riding accident. After Delia's accident, my childhood trauma re-surfaced and I was besieged by nightmares and dissociated memories. Lea helped me re-unite with the little girl I was, whose parents considered anger and reticence to be evidence of being 'naughty' and 'wilful', and thus in need of punishment. Thank you, Lea, for helping me find my way through the red mist of the emotional fires that threatened to consume me as I allowed my memories to re-surface. Thank you for helping me stay the course as I stumbled through a psychiatric wasteland that froze me in my tracks and made me question my own veracity. Thank you for lending me clinical books that helped me understand how trauma affects the brain. I continue to recover from the disabling effects of having been paralysed and overwhelmed with fear. How does one measure finding emotional health, a lucid mind and the joy of being alive in so many ordinary ways? This book is your book too.

The pain of writing this book helped me discover the tenacity and curiosity I had when I was a child. I've lost count of the number of drafts I sent to The Hanbury Agency. Thank you, Maggie Hanbury for your love and interest along the way. I would never have kept writing without you.

When I looked at the moral compass of my childhood world there was no concept of equal rights on any level of Rhodesian society. I believe that every child has a right to feel safe and to learn about social and emotional literacy in a nurturing and inclusive environment. The line between nurture and indoctrination was blurred to the point of their being indistinguishable from one another in my childhood; finding one's way ought to be a voyage of mutual discovery and encouragement - not dictatorship. Thank you, Pathisa Nyathi, for offering me the freedom to share this story. It was heart-breaking not to be able to interact with Africans freely and respectfully. I lost a sense of belonging, together with an essential part of my heart.

I wrote this book for the inmates of Ingutsheni in the hope that their suffering wasn't in vain. I had my freedom at Ingutsheni because Norman Fine was not my psychiatrist – he was my father. His idea of care was never my idea of what it means to care for another person's well-being, nor what it means to be human. The more I faced my fear of him, the more I discovered that my father was just a human being after all, albeit one who was oblivious to the restrictions of his heart and the intransigent perambulations of his mind. If he hadn't been a psychiatrist, I would have been able to forgive him and forget what he did. He, like the psychiatric institution where he worked, hurt a lot more people than just me. I believe that working at Ingutsheni caused my father to lose sight of his humanity. This set me on a painful journey to find my own.

For further information about the history of Zimbabwe and Zimbabwean Culture:

The Grass is Singing and *African Laughter* – Doris Lessing

Surfacing Up: Psychiatry and Social Order in Colonial Zimbabwe, 1908-1968 – Lynette A. Jackson

Malindidzimu: Rhodes Grave - Terence Ranger, with contributions from P. Hubbard, R. Burrett and A. Chennells

Khami – Capital of the Torwa/Butua State - Rob Burrett, Lonke Nyoni and Paul Hubbard

Great Zimbabwe – Spirits, Stones and the Soul of a Nation - Rob S. Burrett and Paul Hubbard

Guy Clutton-Brock: Hero of Zimbabwe – written by his daughter Sally Rosnik

Bulawayo Burning and *Voices from the Rocks* – Terence Ranger

"Rhodesia had an arsenal of dirty tricks. These included the Rhodesian poisons laboratory, which had perfected techniques for the preparation and distribution of poisoned food and poisoned clothes"- Terence Ranger: Journal of Southern African Studies, Volume 18, No 3, September 1992

The Use of Biological Weapons during the Rhodesian War: (2002) Third World Quarterly, 23:6, 1159-1179 - Ian Martinez

"I had knowledge of anthrax from my London days. Anthrax is particularly dangerous because of transmission by spores, which cannot be eliminated by burning or burial. From the Alexander Fleming Hospital in Salisbury, Prime Minister Ian Smith had deliberately spread anthrax spores to cattle and people, I believe in the Lupane and Nkayi area. Enormous numbers of cattle died and some people died upcountry. Reg Austin confirmed to me recently that the anthrax was indeed deliberately spread from the AF

Hospital by the white government. (*This followed the poisoning of wells in South Matabeleland. People and cattle died, scavenging and wild life eg hyenas, vultures, eagles etc feeding on the carcasses also died. There was a swathe of decimation in many villages.)*" Patricia Battye, a social welfare officer in Rhodesia from 1956-1981 in a report shared with the author by Marieke Faber Clarke.

Lozikeyi Dlodlo, Queen of the Ndebele: A very dangerous and intriguing woman – Marieke Faber Clarke and Pathisa Nyathi

Welshman Hadane Mabhena: A Voice for Matabeleland – Marieke Faber Clarke and Pathisa Nyathi

Zimbabwe's Cultural Heritage - Pathisa Nyathi

Prisoners of Rhodesia: Inmates and Detainees in the Struggle 1960-1980 - Munyaradzi B. Munocheseyi

Kalanga Mythology - Herbert Aschwanden

Ndebele Proverbs and Other Sayings - J.N. Pelling

Nervous Conditions - Tsitsi Dangarembga

Children of Wax: A Collection of African folktales from Matabeleland - Alexander McCall-Smith

When Hippo was Hairy and *When Lion Could Fly* – Nick Greaves

Gumiguru - Togara Muzanenhamo

The Rift: A New Africa Breaks Free - Alex Perry

The Boy Next Door – Irene Sabatini

Don't Let's Go to the Dogs Tonight – Alexandra Fuller

We Need New Names – Noviolet Bulawayo